COVID-19 and Social Security Programmes and Schemes in India

COVID-19 and Social Security Programmes and Schemes in India

R. Vasanthagopal
Professor and Director,
School of Distance Education,
University of Kerala, Thiruvananthapuram, Kerala

New Century Publications
New Delhi, India

NEW CENTURY PUBLICATIONS
4800 / 24, Bharat Ram Road,
Ansari Road, Daryaganj,
New Delhi - 110 002 (India)

Tel.: 011 - 4358 7398, 4101 7798, 2324 7798

Email: info@newcenturypublications.com

www.newcenturypublications.com

Editorial office:
4832/24, Ansari Road, Daryaganj,
New Delhi – 110 002

Tel.: 011-4356 0919

First Published: **2020**

ISBN: **978-81-7708-512-9**

Published by New Century Publications and printed at Milan Enterprises, New Delhi.

Designs: Patch Creative Unit, New Delhi.

PRINTED IN INDIA

About the Book

With strong macroeconomic fundamentals, Indian economy was well-placed on the trajectory of steady growth rate when the outbreak of coronavirus epidemic, emanating from China, was reported. On March 11, 2020, the World Health Organization (WHO) declared the epidemic as a pandemic. Normal economic activities around the world came to a screeching halt as governments announced lockdowns to prevent the spread of the disease.

India announced a stringent nationwide lockdown from March 25, 2020. Most of the economic activities in urban areas were halted. However, rural India continued to be normal in view of the exemption from restrictions allowed to farmers to conduct farming operations, including harvesting and transporting their produce to grain markets with the general conditions of face covering, hand hygiene and social distancing.

Sensing the gravity of the situation, Prime Minister Narendra Modi announced, on May 12, 2020, a ₹ 20 lakh crore stimulus package which was about 10 percent of country's gross domestic product (GDP). It was named as *Aatmanirbhar Bharat Abhiyan* (Self-reliant India Initiative).

The details of the ₹ 20 lakh crore package were announced by Finance Minister Nirmala Sitharaman in five tranches during the next five consecutive days. Many of the measures announced by the Government were aimed at giving relief to the poor and lower middle class and increasing the pricing power of farmers.

Over the years, India has built an extensive network of social security programmes and schemes, including the flagship Mahatma Gandhi National Rural Employment Guarantee Scheme (MGNREGS).

This book explains and examines various social security programmes and schemes of the Government of India for the benefit of vulnerable and disadvantaged sections of the society.

About the Author

Dr. R. Vasanthagopal is presently Professor and Director of the School of Distance Education, University of Kerala, Thiruvananthapuram, Kerala. He received his Master of Commerce in Finance from the University of Kerala in 1991. Subsequently, he received his M.Phil. and Ph.D. degrees from the same university in 1993 and 1998 respectively. He joined the University of Kerala as a full professor in 2013. He is an enthusiastic researcher in the areas of commerce, management, finance and human resources management.

Dr. Vasanthagopal has supervised the works of 25 Ph.D. and 12 M.Phil. scholars. He has completed four major research projects sponsored by the University Grants Commission (UGC), New Delhi and Indian Council of Social Science Research (ICSSR), New Delhi. He has published a large number of research articles in national and international journals of repute. He has participated and presented papers at several national and international conferences at home and abroad. He is a reviewer and editorial board member of about 15 reputed research publications.

Contents

Preface

Post-COVID, there has been a tremendous loss of production, income and employment in the Indian economy.

On June 8, 2020, World Bank released its report titled *Global Economic Prospects* and predicted that world economy would shrink by 5.2 percent in 2020. Advanced economies would experience growth falling by 7 percent while emerging economies (including India) as a group would see a growth decline of 2.5 percent. According to the report, Indian economy would shrink by 3.2 percent in the fiscal year 2020-21. The report, which contained an assessment of economic shocks from coronavirus pandemic shutdowns, noted that the pandemic has plunged the world into a severe recession, deepest since the Second World War.

To deal with the economic challenges caused by the pandemic, the Prime Minister announced the creation of 'COVID-19 Economic Response Task Force' under the Union Finance Minister. Similarly, PM CARES Fund was created which deals with any kind of emergency or distress situation like a public health emergency or any other kind of emergency, calamity or distress, either manmade or natural

Prime Minister Narendra Modi announced on May 12, 2020 the Aatmanirbhar Bharat Abhiyan which combined relief, policy reforms and fiscal and monetary measures to help businesses and individuals to cope with the situation created by COVID-19 pandemic. A mega package of ₹ 20 lakh crore (10 percent of GDP) was announced for the purpose.

The details of the ₹ 20 lakh crore package were announced by Finance Minister Nirmala Sitharaman in five tranches during the next five consecutive days. All the measures were aimed at spurring investment and buffering the economy against the Covid pandemic shock.

The first tranche, announced on May 13, 2020, was focused on micro, small and medium enterprises (MSMEs) which were badly hit by the medical crisis.

The second tranche, announced on May 14, 2020, gave relief to the poor and lower middle class.

The third tranche, announced on May 15, 2020, pertained to a mix of financial, legislative and other reform measures aimed largely at increasing the pricing power of farmers.

The fourth tranche, announced on May 16, 2020, related to measures which included a major opening up of coal, defence production, civil aviation, power, space, social infrastructure and atomic energy for private participation.

The fifth tranche, announced on May 17, 2020, focus mainly on Mahatma Gandhi National Rural Employment Guarantee Scheme (MGNREGS)—the flagship rural job guarantee scheme of the Central Government.

Everyone is now agreed that the way forward is too uncertain. It is not possible to clearly see the path over the foreseeable future. It is just not possible to have a precise road map all laid out to be unfolded in one go. Given the unpredictable and volatile international situation, almost every country has to manage under uncertainty. In the circumstances, Government should be prepared to respond to the evolving situation swiftly and effectively, and to the extent possible, in anticipation of immediate developments.

Over the years, India has built an extensive network of social security programmes and schemes, including the flagship Mahatma Gandhi National Rural Employment Guarantee Scheme (MGNREGS). These uniquely Indian versions of automatic stabilizers should protect the vulnerable and disadvantaged sections of society from the extreme impact of COVID pandemic.

Thiruvananthapuram **R. Vasanthagopal**
June 2020

Abbreviations/Acronyms

ALP	Aadhaar Linked Payments
APL	Above Poverty Line
APY	Atal Pension Yojana
BPL	Below Poverty Line
CGFMU	Credit Guarantee Fund for Micro Units
CLTC	City Level Technical Cell
CNAs	Central Nodal Agencies
CSOs	Civil Society Organizations
DBT	Direct Benefit Transfer
DBTL	Direct Benefit Transfer for LPG
DDU-GKY	Deen Dayal Upadhyaya Grameen Kaushalya Yojana
DGRO	District Grievance Redressal Officer
DGT	Directorate General of Training
EMI	Equated Monthly Instalment
EWS	Economically Weaker Section
FCI	Food Corporation of India
FPS	Fair Price Shop
GDP	Gross Domestic Product
GHI	Global Hunger Index
HFA	Housing for All
HFAPoA	Housing for All Plan of Action
HRD	Human Resource Development
HWCs	Health and Wellness Centres
IAF	India Aspiration Fund
ICDS	Integrated Child Development Services
IPRs	Intellectual Property Rights
JAM	Jan Dhan, Aadhaar and Mobile
KCC	Kisan Credit Card
LIG	Low Income Group
LPG	Liquefied Petroleum Gas
MCS	Micro Credit Scheme
MFIs	Micro Finance Institutions

MGNREGA	Mahatma Gandhi National Rural Employment Guarantee Act
MGNREGS	Mahatma Gandhi National Rural Employment Guarantee Scheme
MoRD	Ministry of Rural Development
MSMEs	Micro, Small and Medium Enterprises
MSP	Minimum Support Price
MUDRA	Micro Units Development and Refinance Agency
NABARD	National Bank for Agriculture and Rural Development
NATS	National Apprenticeship Training Scheme
NBA	Nirmal Bharat Abhiyan
NCEUS	National Commission for Enterprises in the Unorganised Sector
NCGTC	National Credit Guarantee Trustee Company
NCS	National Career Service
NeFMS	National Electronic Fund Management System
NGO	Non-governmental Organization
NHP	National Health Policy
NIC	National Informatics Centre
NITI Aayog	National Institution for Transforming India Aayog
NMBS	National Maternity Benefit Scheme
NNMB	National Nutrition Monitoring Bureau
NPCI	National Payment Corporation of India
NPS	National Pension System
NRLM	National Rural Livelihoods Mission
NSDA	National Skill Development Agency
NSDC	National Skill Development Corporation
NSDM	National Skill Development Mission
NULM	National Urban Livelihood Mission
OBCs	Other Backward Classes
PDS	Public Distribution System

PFRDA	Pension Fund Regulatory and Development Authority
PMAY	Pradhan Mantri Aawas Yojana
PMAY-G	Pradhan Mantri Awaas Yojana-Gramin
PMFBY	Pradhan Mantri Fasal Bima Yojana
PMGKY	Pradhan Mantri Garib Kalyan Yojana
PMJAY	Pradhan Mantri Jan Arogya Yojana
PMJDY	Pradhan Mantri Jan Dhan Yojana
PMJJBY	Pradhan Mantri Jeevan Jyoti Bima Yojana
PM-KISAN	Pradhan Mantri Kisan Samman Nidhi
PMKK	Pradhan Mantri Kaushal Kendras
PMKMY	Pradhan Mantri Kisan Maandhan Yojana
PMKVY	Pradhan Mantri Kaushal Vikas Yojana
PMMY	Pradhan Mantri MUDRA Yojana
PMSBY	Pradhan Mantri Suraksha Bima Yojna
PMSMA	Pradhan Mantri Surakshit Matritva Abhiyan
PMUY	Pradhan Mantri Ujjawala Yojana
PPP	Public-Private-Partnership
RAY	Rajiv Awas Yojana
RBI	Reserve Bank of India
RRBs	Regional Rural Banks
SANKALP	Skill Acquisition and Knowledge Awareness for Livelihood Promotion
SCs	Scheduled Castes
SIDBI	Small Industries Development Bank of India
SLTC	State Level Technical Cell
SSDM	State Skill Development Missions
STRIVE	Skill Strengthening for Industrial Value Enhancement
STs	Scheduled Tribes
TPDS	Targeted Public Distribution System
UID	Unique Identification
UTs	Union Territories
WHO	World Health Organization

1

COVID-19 and the Indian Economy

The year 2019 delivered a huge political mandate for the government. Real GDP growth for the year 2019-20 was projected at 7 percent, reflecting a recovery in the economy after a deceleration in the growth momentum throughout 2018-19. The growth in the economy was expected to pick up in 2019-20 as macroeconomic conditions continued to be stable while structural reforms initiated in the previous few years were continuing on course.

On August 23, 2019, Government announced a range of measures to boost economic sentiments, improve availability of credit and working capital and provide some sort of stimulus to the automobile sector. Withdrawal of surcharge on long-term capital gains was also announced.

On August 26, 2019, RBI, in a historic move, transferred ₹ 1.76 lakh crore surplus reserves to the Government. It was meant to help the Government in reducing financial stress on the economy and contain fiscal deficit as well.

On August 28, another package was announced which included liberalization of FDI in coal and digital media.

On August 30, 2019 Government announced the mega merger of public sector banks to modernise the financial sector.

On September 14, 2019, Government announced a package for real estate and export sector. It announced the creation of a ₹ 20,000 crore fund for real estate projects that was expected to help complete around 3,50,000 flats and houses stuck in various stages of completion. Government also announced the introduction of a new scheme for reimbursement of taxes paid on exports. The scheme called the Remission of Duties and Taxes on Export Products came into effect from January 2020, entailing a loss of revenue to the tune of ₹ 50,000.

On September 20, 2019 Government announced a hefty fiscal stimulus for the corporate sector by reducing the corporate tax rate for domestic manufacturing from 30 percent to 22 percent and for new manufacturing companies from 25 percent to 15 percent. The announcement spurred the stock market instantly when BSE Sensex soared 1921 points—the highest single day rise in a decade. The tax cuts became effective retrospectively from April 1, 2019. These tax slashes were expected to allow Indian companies to compete with those in lower-tax jurisdictions globally and also to attract significant investments from abroad.

With all the above favourable factors for rapid economic development, the outbreak of coronavirus epidemic, emanating from China, was reported. On March 11, 2020, the World Health Organization (WHO) declared the COVID-19 epidemic as a pandemic. Normal economic activities around the world started getting disrupted. India announced stringent nationwide lockdown from March 25, 2020.

The lockdown, in consecutive instalments, to slow down the spread of the disease, is expected to affect adversely and sharply the growth rate of the Indian economy during 2020-21 and beyond. There are fears that the economy may actually shrink.

On June 8, 2020, World Bank released its report titled *Global Economic Prospects* and predicted that world economy would shrink by 5.2 percent in 2020. Advanced economies would experience growth falling by 7 percent while emerging economies (including India) as a group would see a growth decline of 2.5 percent. According to the report, Indian economy would shrink by 3.2 percent in the fiscal year 2020-21.

The country is going through an unprecedented crisis owing to Covid pandemic. Nations across the globe have gone into lockdown and people are struggling to find ways to fight the disease and its spread. Social distancing, hand hygiene and face covering have become the new norms of life.

India was one of the first countries to put up a concerted, comprehensive action plan to stop the spread of the virus and limit the number of infections. World Health Organization (WHO) praised the efforts made by the Indian Government to fight the pandemic. India was one of the few countries which announced a complete lockdown even before the Covid cases in the country were less than 1,000. When the medical crisis started, people demonstrated their full commitment in preventing its spread.

To deal with the economic challenges caused by the pandemic, the Prime Minister announced the creation of 'COVID-19 Economic Response Task Force' under the Union Finance Minister. Similarly, PM CARES Fund was created which deals with any kind of emergency or distress situation like a public health emergency or any other kind of emergency, calamity or distress, either manmade or natural

On March 13, 2020, the Central Government announced 4 percent increase in dearness allowance (DA) for its employees and pensioners with effect from January 1, 2020. Considering the calamitous situation created by coronavirus, the Government, on April 23, announced the freezing of DA payment, clarifying that the move was temporary. DA is paid to adjust the cost of living against inflation. Presumably, the Government's intention was to divert a part of available funds at its disposal towards more urgent needs of the corona-stricken and other vulnerable citizens of the country.

Similarly, remuneration of Members of Parliament was reduced by 30 percent for a year.

On May 12, 2020, the Prime Minister announced a ₹ 20 lakh crore stimulus package which was about 10 percent of GDP. It was named as *Aatmanirbhar Bharat Abhiyan* (Self-reliant India Initiative). [1]

The details of the ₹ 20 lakh crore package were announced by Finance Minister Nirmala Sitharaman in five tranches during the next five consecutive days. All the measures were aimed at spurring investment and buffering the economy against the Covid pandemic shock.

Everyone is now agreed that the way forward is too

uncertain. It is not possible to clearly see the path over the foreseeable future. It is just not possible to have a precise road map all laid out to be unfolded in one go. Given the unpredictable and volatile international situation, almost every country has to manage under uncertainty. In the circumstances, Government should be prepared to respond to the evolving situation swiftly and effectively, and to the extent possible, in anticipation of immediate developments.

Similarly, there are indications that protectionist tendencies have increased around the world in anticipation of the growing possibilities of slower growth in advanced economies.

Over the years, India has built an extensive network of social safety-net programmes, including the flagship Mahatma Gandhi National Rural Employment Guarantee Scheme (MGNREGS). These uniquely Indian versions of automatic stabilizers should protect the poor from the extreme impact of Covid pandemic.

Any assessment of the performance of the Indian economy and its current status has to be made in the context of developments in the global economy. India is a major player in international economic affairs, particularly in terms of consumer market. International trade and investment are moderating, trade tensions remain elevated, and financing conditions are tightening. Amid recent episodes of financial stress, growth in emerging market and developing economies has lost momentum. Financial market pressures and trade tensions can escalate, denting global activity.

Compared to other developing economies, India has several strengths that can help mitigate the adverse effects of Covid-induced slowdown. The Government has taken several measures in this direction and the economy is expected to return to the high growth trajectory. Sustained interest in India as a long-term investment destination and a comfortable foreign exchange reserve position suggest that the external sector can continue to support stability and growth. As the monetary and fiscal stimuli work their way through, and if calm and confidence are restored in the global markets, India can see economic turn around.

The high growth *miracle economies* of Asia were able to maintain their high growth for decades despite repeated shocks, as they responded quickly and effectively to counter these shocks through pragmatic policies. There is, therefore, a silver lining for India and a strong case for fast-tracking pending reforms.

Endnote

1. See chapter 2 of this book for *Aatmanirbhar Bharat Abhiyan.*

2

Aatmanirbhar Bharat Abhiyan and the Poor

Prime Minister Narendra Modi announced on May 12, 2020, the *Aatmanirbhar Bharat Abhiyan* (Self-reliant India Initiative) which combined relief, policy reforms and fiscal and monetary measures to help businesses and individuals to cope with the situation created by Covid-19 pandemic. A mega package of ₹ 20 lakh crore (10 percent of GDP) was announced for the purpose. This included ₹ 1.7 lakh crore welfare package announced on March 26, 2020 under the Pradhan Mantri Garib Kalyan Yojana (PMGKY) to provide 3 LPG cylinders free (April, May and June) to over 8 crore beneficiaries of the Pradhan Mantri Ujjawala Yojana (PMUY). It also included monetary measures announced by Reserve Bank of India (RBI) during March-April 2020 which were estimated to be of the order of 5.2 lakh crore.

The details of the ₹ 20 lakh crore package were announced by Finance Minister Nirmala Sitharaman in five tranches during the next five consecutive days. All the measures were aimed at spurring investment and buffering the economy against the Covid pandemic shock.

The first tranche, announced on May 13, 2020, was focused on micro, small and medium enterprises (MSMEs) which were badly hit by the medical crisis.

The second tranche, announced on May 14, 2020, gave relief to the poor and lower middle class.

The third tranche, announced on May 15, 2020, pertained to a mix of financial, legislative and other reform measures aimed largely at increasing the pricing power of farmers.

The fourth tranche, announced on May 16, 2020, related to measures which included a major opening up of coal, defence production, civil aviation, power, space, social infrastructure and atomic energy for private participation.

The fifth tranche, announced on May 17, 2020, focused mainly on Mahatma Gandhi National Rural Employment Guarantee Scheme (MGNREGS)—the flagship rural job guarantee scheme of the Central Government.

2.1 First Tranche Focused on MSMEs

It was particularly challenging time for micro, small and medium enterprises (MSMEs) which were reeling under the harsh impact of the Covid pandemic. With manufacturing units being shut for a considerable period of time and migrant labourers also returning home, many of the MSMEs were on the brink of closing down all operations. In a bid to make this crucial sector of the economy survive, the Finance Minister in her first tranche of the stimulus laid out specific boosters that could offer some relief to this hard-hit sector. The nearly ₹ 6 lakh crore tranche, announced on May 13, 2020, included ₹ 3 lakh crore collateral-free automatic loans for MSMEs.

2.2 Second Tranche for Poor and the Middle Class

Announced on May 14, 2020, it was focused on the poor and lower middle class. It included rental housing facility for migrant workers, free foodgrains for those without ration cards and loan schemes for farmers and street vendors. Following were the elements of the second tranche:

1. Free foodgrains supply to migrants for 2 months. The measure was expected to benefit 8 crore migrants.
2. One nation, one ration card scheme for 67 crore beneficiaries in 23 states, covering 83 percent registered under public distribution scheme (PDS). The scheme will use Aadhaar to allow those entitled to access PDS to draw their quota from anywhere in the country.
3. Interest subsidy of ₹ 1,500 crore under Mudra Shishu loans.
4. Special credit facility of ₹ 5,000 crore for street vendors. The scheme is expected to help 50 lakh vendors.

5. ₹ 6,000 crore employment push for tribals by using funds under Compensatory Afforestation and Planning Authority (CAMPA).
6. Government to launch scheme under PM-Awas Yojana to provide homes at affordable rent to migrant labourers and urban poor.
7. Government-funded housing in cities to be converted into affordable rental housing complexes under public-private-partnership (PPP) mode.
8. ₹ 30,000 crore additional emergency working capital funding through National Bank for Agriculture and Rural Development (NABARD).
9. ₹ 2,00,000 crore concessional credit boost to 2.5 crore farmers through Kisan Credit Cards.
10. Government to extend credit-linked subsidy scheme for middle income group (annual income ₹ 6 to ₹ 18 lakh) housing up to March 2021.

2.3 Third Tranche for Farming Sector

On May 15, 2020, Government announced a mix of financial, legislative and other reform measures aimed largely at increasing the pricing power of farmers. Government proposed to dismantle historical domestic trade barriers to free food and commodities markets with a view to increase the share of farmers' profit in farm income. Government resolved to amend the Essential Commodities Act, 1955, make a central law on agriculture marketing and create a legal framework to provide price assurance to farmers and help improve the quality of their produce. The tranche aggregated to ₹ 1.63 lakh crore.

2.4 Fourth Tranche for Privatization of the Economy

On May 16, 2020 Government announced the fourth set of measures which included a major opening up of coal, defence production, civil aviation, power, space, social infrastructure and atomic energy for private participation. The measures announced were intended to signal India's readiness to proactively seek investment and instil confidence in business circles.

Following were the main elements of the fourth tranche.

1. **Coal:** Government will immediately offer 50 coal mines for commercial mining by private sector without end-use restrictions. The mines will be auctioned on revenue-sharing basis under a simplified regime to increase ease of doing business. Companies can bid even if they do not have experience in coal mining and can sell the output in the open market. Government also announced a ₹ 50,000 crore investment plan for creating infrastructure such as railway tracks and conveyors to evacuate coal from old and new mines.

   Government had earlier approved the promulgation of Mineral Laws (Amendment) Ordinance, 2020 which allowed coal mining by any company present in sectors other than steel and power, and scrapped the captive end-use criterion. Now there is no distinction between captive and non-captive mines.

   It may be recalled that in 2018, the Government had allowed commercial mining by private utilities. The Centre had set a mining target of 1.5 billion tonnes of coal by 2020. Of this, 1 billion tonne was to come from Coal India Limited (CIL) and 0.5 billion tonnes from non-CIL sources.

   With above reforms in place, coal mining has been unshackled from the nationalisation of 1973 and the monopoly of public sector CIL ended. Prior to these reforms, only CIL was allowed to sell coal to end-users.

   It is noteworthy that despite having the world's fourth largest coal reserves, India imports around 235 million tonnes of coal at huge cost in terms of foreign exchange. India's dependence on imports of coal will substantially reduce after these reform measures which have come at a time when global energy scenario is uncertain.

2. **Defence Production:**

- List of weapons/platforms to be notified for import ban. The list of weapons and platforms will be increasingly expanded to boost local manufacturing.
- Promoting indigenisation of spares which are currently imported.
- Corporatisation of ordnance factory board.
- Stock market listing.
- Foreign direct investment (FDI) limit in defence manufacturing raised from the present 49 percent to 74 percent under the automatic route.

3. **Civil Aviation:**

- Easing of restrictions on the use of Indian air space to increase efficiency of passenger aircrafts to save fuel and time. Currently, only 60 percent of domestic airspace is freely available.
- Six more airports to be bid out on public-private-partnership (PPP) basis in second round. Six more in third round.
- Additional investment by private players in 12 airports expected to be ₹ 13,000 crore.
- India to become global hub for maintenance, repair and overhaul.

4. **Power Sector:**

- Tariff policy reforms.
- Direct benefit transfer (DBT) for subsidy.
- Smart pre-paid metres.
- Time-bound grant of open access.
- Distribution companies (Discoms) to be penalised for load shedding.
- Electricity distribution utilities or power departments in the Union Territories (UTs) will be privatised for better service and efficiency.

5. **Space:** Private firms to be allowed in the field of satellites and other space-based services.

- Private sector to be allowed to use Indian Space Research Organization (ISRO) facilities.

6. **Social Infrastructure:** Government's share in viability gap funding for development of social infrastructure, including hospitals, raised from 20 percent to 30 percent, with a total outlay of ₹ 8,100 crore.
7. **Atomic Energy:** Research reactor to be set up in PPP mode for production of medical isotopes.

2.5 Fifth Tranche Focused on MGNREGS

On May 17, 2020, Government announced the fifth and the final tranche of policy reforms and fiscal incentives. The main focus was on Mahatma Gandhi National Rural Employment Guarantee Scheme (MGNREGS)—the flagship rural job guarantee scheme of the Central Government. In the budget for 2020-21, an allocation of ₹ 61,000 crore was made for the scheme. With millions of daily wagers and others returning to their villages in the wake of Covid-19 pandemic, there has been a surge in demand for work in rural areas. Hence, Government announced, as part of the fifth tranche, an additional allocation of ₹ 40,000 crore for MGNREGS. Original allocation and additional allocation make for ₹ 1,01,000 crore, making MGNREGS the only social welfare programme in the country with a kitty of ₹ 1,00,000 crore or more. MGNREGS has emerged as the backbone of rural income for the poor. It guarantees 100 days of work for one person in a year. The wage rate is ₹ 202 per day. There are demands to increase this limit to 150 days.

Other components of the fifth tranche were as under:

1. A substantial hike in the borrowing limit for states from 3 percent to 5 percent of gross state domestic product (GSDP) for the current fiscal year, subject to their carrying out specific reforms.
2. A new plan to end the monopoly of public sector enterprises (PSEs) and open up sectors for private participation. For the sake of public interest, a minimum of

one and a maximum of four PSEs will continue to operate.
3. Substantial ease of compliance for businesses, including relaxations in the insolvency and bankruptcy framework.
4. Creation of a robust public health infrastructure covering districts and blocks.
5. Launch of a digital education programme.
6. Initiative for mental health and emotional well-being of teachers, students and families.

On May 17, 2020 Finance Minister said that the Government has provided ₹ 11,02,650 crore stimulus in the five tranches. Earlier, stimulus worth ₹ 9,94,403 crore was infused in the system through fiscal policy measures that included ₹ 1,70,000 crore relief package on May 26 and ₹ 8,01,603 crore monetary measures by the RBI since March 27 (Table 2.1).

Table 2.1: Aatmanirbhar Package at a Glance

(₹ crore)

Scheme/Tranche	Date	Amount
Earlier measures, of which:	...	**9,94,403**
PM Garib Kalyan Yojana	March 26, 2020	1,70,000
Reserve Bank of India (RBI) monetary measures	March-April, 2020	8,01,603
Five tranches	May 13 to 17, 2020	**11,02,650**
Grand Total		**20,97,053**

2.6 Assessment of Aatmanirbhar Bharat Package

Various relief and reform measures announced by the Government were hailed as radical and historic by economists. They were as structural in nature as the ones announced in the early 1990s. The then Government led by Prime Minister Narsimha Rao forced to liberalize and open up the Indian economy in the face of acute balance of payment crisis.

In the present case, the stimulus for reforms to *unshackle* the economy was provided by the crisis created by Covid pandemic. In fact, the Government seized the crisis to push forward long-pending industrial and other economic reforms in an atmosphere of least political resistance.

Whatever may have been the circumstances leading to these drastic reforms, they were steps in the right direction considering the changed and changing global realities. Post-Covid, uncertainty is reigning supreme and countries are thinking of self-sufficiency. World economies are unsure as to what extent they can depend on others in the future. Global firms are reducing their presence in China and relocating to other countries, shifting the supply chain in the process. The world is not going to be the same. The working environment (e.g. working from home) will change and so also the inter-personal contacts for business.

As in the case of announcing lockdowns, India is quite early to have taken the cue of self-sufficiency.

2.7 Pradhan Mantri Garib Kalyan Rojgar Abhiyan

On June 20, 2020, Prime Minister Narendra Modi launched a ₹ 50,000 crore rural jobs programme named as Pradhan Mantri Garib Kalyan Rojgar Abhiyan. It is aimed at creating livelihoods for jobless migrant workers who moved back from the cities to their home villages during the lockdown imposed to stop the spread of coronavirus pandemic.

This initiative will offer 125 days of employment in 116 districts across six states which witnessed large scale reverse migration of workers from the cities, triggering a livelihood crisis. The six states are Bihar, Uttar Pradesh, Madhya Pradesh, Rajasthan, Jharkhand and Odisha.

3

Poverty and Global Hunger Index (GHI), 2019

The final objective of all economic efforts is human development which encompasses quality of life, the level of well-being and access to basic social services. The Fundamental Rights that India's Constitution guarantees to every citizen include the right to life and the right to livelihood is inherent in the right to life.

3.1 Poverty in India

The root cause of social insecurity in India is poverty and that is largely due to lack of adequate or productive employment opportunities. It is described as chronic or structural social insecurity, arising from insufficient degree of overall economic development. It is associated with other insecurities emanating from conventional contingencies such as the loss of employment, disability, old age, death etc. which are called the *second-order* type of insecurities or conventional social insecurity.

The provision of adequate and stable incomes will enable the poor to satisfy their basic needs. Till then, the State has to assume the basic responsibility of providing social security, especially in respect of those contingencies which would be difficult for individuals to cover without assistance from the state. The State also has the responsibility to provide the means of livelihood to those who cannot work and earn their living due to childhood, old age or other infirmities.

Poverty is a widespread social evil in underdeveloped countries of the world, particularly in Asia and Africa. There is no standard definition of poverty for all the countries of the world. Being a relative concept, the meaning of poverty differs from country to country. The concept, causes and incidence of poverty in India are discussed below.

3.1.1 Meaning of Poverty Line: In India, poverty is defined in terms of a minimum (subsistence) level of living rather than a reasonable level of living. Thus, minimum physical quantities of cereals, pulses, clothing etc. are determined for a subsistence level. These physical quantities are multiplied by their prices and converted into monetary terms, determining the per capita consumption/income for subsistence level. Persons whose income/consumption is below this determined figure are considered to be below the poverty line.

Thus, poverty line is based on the definition of a norm which takes nutritional requirements into account and all persons below the norm are classified as poor. More specifically, the level of consumption below which people are living in poverty is set by determining the overall expenditure level at which consumers could purchase a food intake of 2,400 calories in rural areas or 2,100 calories in urban areas, which was estimated as the minimum necessary food intake. This overall expenditure sum was evaluated for a base period in 1979 and is updated from time-to-time using price indices.

3.1.2 Causes of Poverty: Widespread poverty in India is attributable to a host of factors, viz. population explosion, lack of industrialisation, failure of land reforms and failure of fiscal policy to narrow the gap between the rich and the poor.

Industrial development of the country has neither been on desirable lines nor at expected rate. Undue emphasis on capital-intensive industries has failed to generate sufficient jobs for the labour force.

Land reforms programme was started with great fanfare soon after Independence. However, it has failed to achieve the desired results. The incidence of poverty in rural areas is mainly due to the failure of land reforms.

Similarly, taxation and expenditure policies of the government have not been used effectively to bridge the gap between the rich and the poor.

Poverty in India is a chronic and multi-dimensional phenomenon. There is geography of poverty, with poverty being concentrated in the rural areas of certain states. There is sociology of poverty, with certain social groups suffering the most. There are identifiable occupational features of the poor. They are concentrated in agricultural labour and artisanal households in rural areas, and among casual labourers in urban areas. Casual labourers in urban areas are essentially distress migrants from rural areas in states where agricultural land-man ratio is very adverse, and where agricultural incomes have not been growing

3.1.3 Incidence of Poverty: From the statistical and other information available on the subject, the following facts emerge regarding the geo-social aspects of poverty in India.

1. Incidence of poverty is more in rural areas than in urban areas.
2. Incidence of poverty is the greatest among small farmers and landless workers in rural areas.
3. Poverty in urban areas is largely the overflow of rural poor into the urban areas.
4. Urban poverty is concentrated in the casual labour households.
5. Wide inter-state disparities are visible in the poverty ratios. Uttar Pradesh, Bihar, Madhya Pradesh, Odisha and Rajasthan account for most of the poor in India.
6. Among the social groups, scheduled castes, scheduled tribes and backward castes account for more percentage of the poor than their share in the population.

Poverty eradication may either be left to the automatic mechanism of growth process and/or to programmes aimed at direct assault on poverty. The initial thinking of the Government relied on the automatic benefits of growth coupled with a progressive taxation policy. However, this strategy did not work on desired lines. The equity objective was sought to be pursued through redistribution of assets. However, land reforms could not be implemented effectively.

The problem of poverty could not be tackled through growth, which itself was slow over a long period of time. Hence, direct intervention through poverty alleviation programmes became necessary. Lately, the Government has increasingly resorted to direct attack on poverty through rural development and rural employment schemes.

The socio-economically disadvantaged are yet to benefit from economic reforms. The challenge to overcome the scourge of poverty remains a daunting task. The support of the poor for reforms and their involvement in the development process can be achieved only if they start benefiting from the policies. It is necessary to ensure that the poor and the deprived have greater stake in economic reforms than at present for mobilising their enthusiastic participation in the development process. Economic reforms must be guided by compassion and distributive justice. Improvement of living conditions of the poorest and the weakest sections of society should be high priority areas.

3.2 Global Hunger Index (GHI), 2019 and India

3.2.1 What is GHI: GHI Report, 2019 was prepared jointly by Concern Worldwide, an Irish aid agency, and Welt Hunger Hilfe, a German organisation.

GHI is a tool designed to comprehensively measure and track hunger at global, regional, and national levels. GHI scores are calculated each year to assess progress and setbacks in combating hunger. The GHI is designed to raise awareness and understanding of the struggle against hunger, provide a way to compare levels of hunger between countries and regions, and call attention to those areas of the world where hunger levels are highest and where the need for additional efforts to eliminate hunger is greatest.

GHI ranks countries on a 100-point scale, with 0 being the best score (no hunger) and 100 being the worst. Values less than 10 reflect low hunger, values from 20 to 34.9 indicate serious hunger, values from 35 to 49.9 are alarming and values of 50 or more are extremely alarming.

GHI calculates the levels of hunger and under-nutrition worldwide. The four indicators for the index are: (a) under-nourishment, (b) child stunting, (c) child wasting (low weight for height) and (d) child mortality.

Commitment to reach Zero Hunger by 2030 is a fundamental ambition of the Sustainable Development Goals,

The Report warned that climate change was causing alarming levels of hunger and making it more difficult to feed people in the world's most vulnerable regions.

17 countries which had a score of less than five (that is their levels of hunger were very low) were not given individual ranks but were ranked collectively (Table 3.1).

Table 3.1 also shows the ranks and scores achieved by China, Sri Lanka, Nepal, Bangladesh, Pakistan and India. The country with the severest problem of hunger at rank 117 with a score of 53.6 was the Central African Republic.

Table 3.1: Global Hunger Index (GHI) Ranks and Scores, 2019: Select Countries

The following 17 countries which had a score of less than five (i.e. their levels of hunger were very low) were not given individual ranks but were ranked collectively: Belarus, Bosnia & Herzegovina, Bulgaria, Chile, Costa Rica, Croatia, Cuba, Estonia, Kuwait, Latvia, Lithuania, Montenegro, Romania, Slovak Republic, Turkey, Ukraine and Uruguay		
Country	**Rank**	**Score**
China	25	6.5
Sri Lanka	66	17.1
Nepal	73	20.8
Bangladesh	88	25.8
Pakistan	94	28.5
India	**102**	**30.3**
Central African Republic	117	53.6

Source: Global Hunger Index, 2019.

3.2.2 GHI and India: India was classified as a country with *serious* levels of hunger according to the GHI,

2019. India was ranked 102 out of 117 countries in terms of severity of hunger.

India slipped from 95th rank in 2010 to 102nd in 2019 on GHI. In 2000, India's rank was 83rd out of 113 countries.

India's 102nd rank in 2019 meant that there were only 15 other countries in this index which were worse-off than India. Nearly all these were African countries: Sierra Leone, Uganda, Djibouti, Congo, Sudan, Afghanistan, Zimbabwe, Timor-Leste, Haiti, Liberia, Zambia, Madagascar, Chad, Yemen and Central African Republic.

The poor performance of the country between 2010 and 2019 was attributed mainly to the increase in prevalence of wasting among children under five. Child wasting in India was the highest rate of wasting for any country in the Report at 20.8 percent. Even conflict-ridden Yemen and climate crisis-hit Djibouti fared better than India on that front. According to the Report, just 9.6 percent of all children in India between 6 and 23 months of age are fed a minimum acceptable diet.

It is noteworthy that the official National Family Health Survey of 2015-16 also put the prevalence of wasting in India at 21 percent. Gujarat, Jharkhand, Karnataka, Madhya Pradesh, and Maharashtra were the big states that contributed to the high wasting percentage in the country.

However, there was an improvement in India's GHI score. The improvement from 38.9 in 2005 to 32 in 2010 was followed by a change from 32 to 30.3 between 2010 and 2019. India demonstrated an improvement in indicators such as under-5 mortality rate, prevalence of stunting among children, and prevalence of under-nourishment owing to inadequate food.

The report made a mention of the Swachh Bharat campaign but said that it had not worked well enough, despite being important: "Even with new latrine construction, however, open defecation is still practiced. This situation jeopardises the population's health and consequently, children's growth and development as their ability to absorb nutrients is compromised".

3.2.3 Definitions:

A. Hunger: The problem of hunger is complex, and different terms are used to describe its various forms. Hunger is usually understood to refer to the distress associated with a lack of sufficient calories. The Food and Agriculture Organization of the United Nations (FAO) defines food deprivation, or under-nourishment, as the consumption of too few calories to provide the minimum amount of dietary energy that each individual requires to live a healthy and productive life, given that person's sex, age, stature, and physical activity level.

B. Under-nutrition: Under-nutrition goes beyond calories and signifies deficiencies in any or all of the following: energy, protein, and/or essential vitamins and minerals. Under-nutrition is the result of inadequate intake of food in terms of either quantity or quality, poor utilization of nutrients due to infections or other illnesses, or a combination of these immediate causes. These, in turn, are caused by a range of underlying factors, including household food insecurity; inadequate maternal health or childcare practices; or inadequate access to health services, safe water, and sanitation.

C. Malnutrition: Malnutrition refers more broadly to both under-nutrition (problems caused by deficiencies) and over-nutrition (problems caused by unbalanced diets, such as consuming too many calories in relation to requirements with or without low intake of micronutrient-rich foods).

D. Over-nutrition: Over-nutrition, resulting in overweight, obesity, and non-communicable diseases, is becoming increasingly common throughout the world, with implications for human health, government expenditures, and food systems development. While over-nutrition is an important concern, the GHI focuses specifically on issues relating to under-nutrition.

4

Social Justice and Social Security

India's development efforts since Independence in 1947 have not benefited different social groups equitably. Certain social groups such as the scheduled castes (SCs), scheduled tribes (STs), other backward classes (OBCs) and minorities (particularly Muslims) have historically been disadvantaged and vulnerable. Then there are certain other groups which are often discriminated against and which suffer from handicaps. These include persons with disabilities, older persons, street children, beggars, victims of substance abuse.

The concept of inclusive growth demands that all social groups have equal access to the services provided by the State and equal opportunity for upward economic and social mobility. It is also necessary to ensure that there is no discrimination against any section of society. The Constitution of India contains various provisions for the development of such marginalized groups. Their individual and collective growth, however, cannot be ensured without improving their surroundings and providing clean drinking water, toilets and educational opportunities.

4.1 Social Justice

The objective of social justice is the attainment of social health which implies the realisation of such objectives as adequate living standards, opportunities for cultural development through individual and group self-expressions, and re-adjustment of human relations leading to social harmony. A comprehensive concept of living standards includes the satisfaction of basic needs like food, clothing and shelter as well as normal satisfactions of family life, enjoyment of physical and mental health, opportunities for the expression of skills and recreational abilities, and active and pleasurable social participation.

The achievement of social justice demands co-operative and concerted effort on the part of the State and the people. These objectives are to be achieved mainly by revitalising the nation's life by creating well-organised and active regional communities in rural and urban areas to work co-operatively for national development. Such decentralised community groups should release national energy, extend the scope for leadership, and help to create initiative and organisation extensively in the remotest parts of the country.

The aim of social welfare in the past was essentially curative, and efforts were directed towards relief for the handicapped and the uplift of the under-privileged sections of society. It is essential to maintain vigilance over weaknesses and strains in the social structure and remedy the deficiencies by organising social service programmes/schemes. The aim of all social policies now is the gradual rehabilitation of all weak, handicapped and anti-social elements in society.

Social justice (inclusive growth) is a multi-dimensional concept. Inclusive growth should result in lower incidence of poverty, broad-based and significant improvement in health outcomes, universal access for children to school, increased access to higher education and improved standards of education, including skill development. It should also be reflected in better opportunities for both wage employment and livelihood, and in improvement in provision of basic amenities like water, electricity, roads, sanitation and housing.

Particular attention needs to be paid to the needs of the SC/ST and OBC population. Women and children deserve special attention in terms of the reach of relevant schemes in many sectors. Minorities and other excluded groups also need special programmes to bring them into the mainstream. To achieve inclusiveness in all these dimensions requires multiple interventions, and success depends not only on introducing new policies and government programmes, but on institutional and attitudinal changes brought about, which take time.

In short, social justice is necessarily a slow process. Its principal limitations relate to: (a) financial resources which can be spared for social services, (b) lack of trained personnel and organisations devoted to social welfare and (c) lack of reliable data pertaining to social problems. These factors tend to limit the immediate objectives of social justice to groups which are in a vulnerable position or need special assistance.

4.2 Social Security

Social security refers to public assistance in all cases of underserved want. It provides human security to the poor and the destitute.

The social security situation in India is characterised by ambiguity in policy and responsibility. There is a variety of schemes but these have been framed at various points of time and, therefore, do not conform to any overall design reflecting a comprehensive and consistent policy or direction.

The pattern of economic development in India since Independence in 1947 has left in its trail a variety of inequalities which have caused socio-politico tensions. While the economy has performed well in terms of growth rate of gross domestic product (GDP), its performance in terms of human development indicators has been unsatisfactory.

India's recent economic growth performance has, indeed, been creditable. However, such growth must make a demonstrable difference to the lives of the poorest and most vulnerable citizens. India has the potential and the means to secure a reasonable standard of living for all of its citizens. The socio-economically disadvantaged—particularly women in rural areas—are yet to benefit from development efforts.

Development and empowerment of scheduled castes (SCs), scheduled tribes (STs), other backward classes (OBCs), minorities, disabled and other social groups in order to bring them at par with the rest of society is a commitment enshrined in the Constitution. Policies of the Central and State Governments have tried to ensure equal rights, and access to benefits and resources to disadvantaged groups in society to enable them to develop their potential and capacities as agents of social change, through the process of planned development.

4.2.1 Need for Social Security: Economic growth alone cannot be relied upon to deal either with the promotion, or with the protection of living standards. Many view social security as a system of proper distribution of income and also a right mechanism of wage fixation. Social security is an essential ingredient in the protection, development and full utilisation of human resources.

Millions of people in developing countries live on the edge of disaster. Even in industrial countries people are constantly at risk from crime or violence of unemployment. Joblessness is a major source of insecurity, undermining people's entitlement to income and other benefits. For too long the ideal of security has referred to military security or the security of states. One of the most basic needs is security of livelihood, but people also want to be free from chronic threats, such as disease or repression, as well as from sudden and hurtful disruptions in their daily lives.

4.2.2 Social Security in India's Constitution: The Fundamental Rights that India's Constitution guarantees to every citizen include the right to life, and as the Supreme Court has pointed out, the right to livelihood is inherent in the right to life. The ultimate object of social security is to ensure that everyone has the means of livelihood. It follows, therefore, that the right to social security is also inherent in the right to life. According to the Supreme Court of India, India is constitutionally a socialist state. The principal aim of socialism is to eliminate inequality of income and status and to provide a decent standard of living to the working people.

Part IV of the Constitution contains the Directive Principles of State Policy. Some of these Directive Principles which deal with social security and welfare of disadvantaged groups are as under:

1. The State shall strive to promote the welfare of the people

by securing and protecting, as effectively as it may, a social order in which justice, social, economic and political, shall inform all the institutions of the national life. The State shall, in particular, strive to minimum inequalities in income, and endeavour to eliminate inequalities in status, facilities and opportunities not only amongst individuals, but also amongst groups of people residing in different areas or engaged in different vocations (Article 38).

2. The State shall, in particular, direct its policy towards securing: (a) that the citizens, men and women equally, have the right to an adequate means to livelihood, (b) that the ownership and control of the material resources of the community are so distributed as best to sub-serve the common good, (c) that the operation of the economic system does not result in the concentration of wealth and means of production to the common detriment, (d) that there is equal pay for equal work for both men and women, (e) that the health and strength of workers, men and women, and the tender age of children are not abused and that citizens are not forced by economic necessity to enter avocations unsuited to their age or strength and (f) that children are given opportunities and facilities to develop in a healthy manner and in conditions of freedom and dignity and that childhood and youth are protected against exploitation and against moral and material abandonment (Article 39).
3. The State shall, within the limits of its economic capacity and development, make effective provision for securing the right to work, to education and to public assistance in cases of unemployment, old age, sickness and disablement, and in other cases of under-served want (Article 41).
4. The State shall endeavour to secure, by suitable legislation or economic organization or in any other way, to all workers, agricultural, industrial or otherwise, work, a

living wage, conditions of work ensuring a decent standard of life and full enjoyment of leisure and social and cultural opportunities (Article 43).

5. The State shall promote with special care the educational and economic interests of the weaker sections of the people, and in particular, of the Scheduled Castes and the Scheduled Tribes and shall protect them from social injustice and all forms of exploitation (Article 46).

Recognising the special needs of the weaker sections, the Constitution of India not only guarantees them equality before the law (Article 14) but also enjoins the State to make special provisions of affirmative discrimination for the advancement of any socially and educationally backward classes, scheduled castes (SCs) and scheduled tribes (STs) [Article 15(4)]. It also empowers the State to make provision for reservation in appointments or posts in favour of any backward class citizens [Article 16(4)].

The Constitution of India also states categorically that untouchability is abolished and its practice in any form is forbidden (Article 17).

For promoting the welfare of STs and for raising the level of administration of the Scheduled Areas to that of the rest of the State (Article 244), special financial assistance is ensured under the Constitution [Article 275(1)]. Reservation of seats for SCs and STs in the democratic institutions (Articles 330 and 332), educational institutions and in services (Article 335) is another measure of positive discrimination in favour of these groups.

With regard to the welfare and development of minorities, the Constitution incorporates certain safeguards to recognise their rights in conserving their culture and establish and administer educational institutions of their choice (Articles 29 and 30).

In the light of the above, no one can argue that the Indian Constitution does not visualise a regime of social security for the citizens in general, and the workforce in particular. In fact, as long as these Principles and Fundamental Rights remain in the Constitution, the Indian State, and the policies of any government that may be in power, will be judged by their commitment to these Principles and Rights. Changes in policy cannot abrogate the responsibility of the State in this area.

Moreover, it does not seem likely that any proposal to amend the Constitution to abridge or dilute these Rights and Principles will get the requisite popular or parliamentary mandate. As long as these are part of the Constitution, one cannot overlook them or depart from them. No political party or responsible thinker has suggested the deletion or dilution of these commitments in the Constitution.

4.2.3 Fundamental Rights versus Directive Principles of State Policy: It has been rightly pointed out that the Directive Principles are not justiceable, and therefore they do not have the same force as the Fundamental Rights. It has also been pointed out that the difference in the status that has been accorded in the Constitution to Fundamental Rights and Directive Principles was not the result of difference in degrees of faith or commitment, but of the belief that the financial implications of making the Directive Principles justiceable could not be laid on the state all of a sudden, that the responsibility for implementation had to be matched with the accrual or acquisition of the requisite financial resources, and that there was, therefore, an inevitable need to provide for gradualness.

Fundamental Rights and Directive Principles leave no doubt about the concern and commitment of the Constitution to the right of citizens to enjoy social security that the security that is envisaged is not only against aggression and violation of sovereignty by other countries, but also security against deprivation. The concept of social security and the commitment to social security are thus implicit in the Constitution. The judgements of the Supreme Court that clearly declare that the right to life includes the right to livelihood should remove any doubt about the commitment to social security. The right to livelihood includes the right to work, and the right to education that equips the citizens with the skills that they need for employment as well as the ability to fulfil their civic and social responsibilities.

To sum up, the constitutional commitments made in favour of socially disadvantaged groups prompted the policy makers and the planners to accord high priority for the welfare and development of these groups right from the country's First Five Year Plan launched on April 1, 1951. During the 1950s, the general developmental programmes were so designed as to cater adequately to the backward classes. Efforts were also made to ensure that the benefits of economic development accrued more and more to the relatively less privileged classes of the society in order to reduce inequalities. Successive Five Year Plans have sought to raise the socio-economic levels of all the people including scheduled castes/scheduled tribes and other weaker sections.

In spite of Constitutional Directives and a number of legislative and executive measures by the Government, the conditions of socially disadvantaged groups have not improved appreciably mainly due to the lack of economic support. Although special programmes have been formulated in the Five Year Plans for their socio-economic development, the basic problem of their poor economic base has remained almost untouched so far.

Continuing to pursue traditional occupations, they are unable to avail of the fruits of economic growth and participate fully in the process of modernisation. Even the few educated groups amongst them are unable to compete for job opportunities created while scheduled tribes still remain largely outside the main stream of development mainly because of their relative isolation and their exploitation by outside agencies. A large proportion of bonded labourers are also scheduled castes. In both these cases, social and economic impoverishment merges to form a single basic factor for backwardness.

In short, development efforts since Independence in 1947

have not had the desired impact on these socially, economically and educationally handicapped groups. Their problems cannot be resolved through the percolation of general economic growth. The majority of SCs/STs—who form one-fourth of the population—are below the poverty line and also face special problems peculiar to them.

5

Mahatma Gandhi National Rural Employment Guarantee Scheme (MGNREGS)

Mahatma Gandhi National Rural Employment Guarantee Act (MGNREGA) was enacted by Parliament in 2005. MGNREGA was notified on September 7, 2005. The Act states that "the objective of the legislation is to enhance the livelihood security of poor households in rural areas". MGNREGA was operationalized through the Mahatma Gandhi National Rural Employment Guarantee Scheme (MGNREGS) with effect from February 2, 2006 when 200 selected districts of the country were brought under its purview (Phase I, 2006-07). MGNREGA was extended to additional 130 districts in Phase II during 2007-08. The remaining rural areas were notified with effect from April 1, 2008.

5.1 Objectives and Significance of MGNREGS

The objective of the MGNREGS is to enhance the livelihood security of unorganised workers in rural areas by guaranteeing 100 days of wage employment in a financial year to a rural household whose members volunteer to do unskilled manual work. It further aims at creating durable assets and strengthening the livelihood resource base of the rural poor. The choice of works suggested in the scheme address causes of chronic poverty like drought, deforestation, soil erosion, etc. so that the process of employment generation is on a sustainable basis.

The significance of MGNREGS lies in the fact that it creates a right-based framework for wage employment programmes and makes the Government legally bound to provide employment to those who seek it. In this way the scheme goes beyond providing a social safety net, and guarantees the right to employment. By prioritizing natural resource management and emphasizing the creation of durable assets it holds the potential of becoming a growth engine for sustainable development of an agriculture-based economy.

Under MGNREGS, employment is dependent upon the worker exercising the choice to apply for registration, obtain a job card and then to seek employment through a written application for the time and duration chosen by him/her. The legal guarantee has to be fulfilled within the time limit prescribed and this mandate is underpinned by the provision of unemployment allowance. The scheme is thus designed to offer an incentive structure to the States for providing employment as ninety percent of the cost for employment provided is borne by the Centre, and there is a concomitant disincentive for not providing employment, if demanded, as the States then bear the double indemnity of unemployment and the cost of unemployment allowance. Earlier wage employment programmes were allocation based.

However, MGNREGS is not supply driven but demand driven. Resource transfer under MGNREGS is based on the demand for employment and this provides another critical incentive to States to leverage the scheme to meet the employment needs of the poor. The delivery system has been made accountable, as it envisages an Annual Report on the outcomes of MGNREGS to be presented by the Central Government to the Parliament and to the State Legislature by the State Government.

5.2 Expression of Demand for Employment

Since MGNREGS is a right-based programme, expression of demand for employment by the rural poor is the basic premise of its operation, especially if the wage seekers are illiterate and unorganized. Generating awareness about the programme among local rural communities becomes critical for enabling the rural poor to express demand. States have adopted various methods for communication and social mobilisation that include preparation of communication material on MGNREGS processes in simple local language, orientation of sarpanches/ward members, convening gram sabhas, using district teams for village level interactions, local vernacular newspapers, TV and radio spots, pamphlets and brochures, local cultural forums, fixing a Rozgar Day in a week and establishing a helpline. The full knowledge of the rights that MGNREGS confers on the rural poor is the most important pre-requisite to enable them to seek employment as per their choice of time and duration.

5.3 Labour Budget, Inventory of Projects and Perspective Plan

MGNREGS guarantees providing employment within 15 days of demand and the instrument for providing employment is unskilled manual work selected from the list of permissible works. This legal guarantee has implication for the way in which works have to be planned.

A labour budget is required to be prepared to facilitate advance planning, whereby districts estimate their labour demand for the ensuing financial year by December end. National guidelines indicate the way in which the annual shelf of projects may be prepared to meet the estimated labour demand. Districts should keep a list of works ready to meet employment demand. Estimated benefits in terms of person days need to be assessed, so that the employment expected to be generated through the works planned may be clearly matched with the estimated employment demand. Physical improvement envisaged (land/water conservation etc.) has to be quantified so that the focus remains on creating durable and productive assets that support further self-sustaining employment. Displaying the list of approved works at the Gram Panchayat Office and the details of works taken up on the work site has been stipulated so that the workers know the work opportunities locally available.

National guidelines lay down the broad principles of preparing a Five Year District Perspective Pan that must have the following components: (a) village mapping of natural resources and social infrastructure, (b) identification of gaps and works that can be taken up as per MGNREGS permissible list, (c) assessment of works that respond to what local people want, (d) what will build a livelihood base to enable them to move out of MGNREGS to sustainable employment and (e) assessment of labour demand.

5.4 Work Record, Payment of Wages and Preventing Bogus Muster Rolls

The legal guarantee of MGNREGS mandates that wages due to workers be paid within 15 days of work completion. This requires that a fair record be maintained for the work done. To ensure that authentic muster rolls are used, numbered muster rolls are to be issued for each sanctioned work by programme officer and maintained on the work site by the executing agency. Muster rolls must mention job card numbers of workers, days worked, quantum of work done, amount paid and must have space for recording inspections.

Muster rolls should be read out on the work site during measurement and wage payment to prevent bogus records. Entries of the muster roll should be correspondingly recorded in the job cards of the workers. Updating of muster roll data at the block level computers in a 15 days cycle needs to be ensured. Regular measurement and supervision of works should be done by qualified technical personnel on time.

5.5 Vigilance and Transparency

Vigilance and transparency have been strongly emphasized in MGNREGS. The field verification of MGNREGS processes is through external and internal agencies and the feedback is shared with the States for follow up. Independent concurrent studies have also been taken up. Monitoring at the State level is required and States are expected to ensure 100 percent verification at block level, 10 percent at district level and 2 percent at the state level, especially of work muster rolls, and records. Guidelines for muster roll verification have been evolved. The setting up and training local vigilance and monitoring committees is also required for bringing in lateral transparency.

A web-enabled MIS www.nrega.nic.in has been developed that seeks to place all information in public domain. It is a household level database and has internal checks for ensuring consistency and conformity to normative processes. All critical parameters get monitored in public domain. Since the MIS places all critical data on the web and this data is software engineered, it has significant advantages in terms of transparency as it allows cross verification of records and generation of reports on any parameter of the Act.

5.6 Other Processes of MGNREGS

5.6.1 Right-based Framework:

1. Adult members of a rural household who are willing to do unskilled manual work may apply for registration to the local Gram Panchayat, in writing, or orally.
2. Gram Panchayat after due verification will issue a job card. The job card will bear the photograph of all adult members of the household and is free of cost.
3. A job card holding household may submit a written application for employment to the Gram Panchayat, stating the time and duration for which work is sought.

5.6.2 Women Empowerment: MGNREGS stipulates that priority shall be given to women. In terms of implementation, it mandates that a minimum of one-third of the beneficiaries shall be women who have registered and have requested for work.

5.6.3 Public Accountability: MGNREGS contains specific provisions for public accountability. This has to be accomplished through the provisions made in MGNREGA and guidelines regarding right to information, proactive disclosure of information and a transparent social audit process. The right to information should be followed in both letter and spirit in all matters relating to MGNREGS. Section 17 of MGNREGA provides for social audit of all works in a *gram panchayat* by the *gram sabha* and the

Gram Panchayat has to provide records for social audit.

5.6.4 Grievance Redressal: Enforcement of the right to employment requires setting up an effective grievance redressal system. MGNREGS vests the responsibility for grievance redressal with the programme officer. To ensure prompt grievance redressal, certain basic arrangements must be ensured, such as setting up a grievance redressal cell at the Programme Officer (PO)/District Programme Co-ordinator (DPC) offices, preferably with a toll free helpline. The PO and DPC must review the disposal of complaints on a monthly basis and the persons concerned must be informed.

5.6.5 Financial Management: A non-lapsable Central Employment Guarantee Fund has been set up to ensure that availability of funds match working season demands. Districts have dedicated accounts for MGNREGS funds and submit their proposals based on clearly delineated guidelines so that funds may be devolved efficiently at each level, and adequate funds may be available to respond to demand. The funds are released on the basis of demand for employment received in a district and are based on an appraisal of both financial and physical indicators of outcomes.

5.6.6 Time-bound Guarantee:

1. Gram Panchayat will issue a dated receipt of the written application for employment, against which the guarantee of providing employment within 15 days operates. If employment is not provided within 15 days, daily unemployment allowance in cash has to be paid. Liability of payment of unemployment allowance is of the States.
2. Work should ordinarily be provided within 5 kilometre radius of the village or else extra wages of 10 percent are payable
3. Wages are to be paid according to minimum wages. Disbursement of wages has to be done on weekly basis and not beyond a fortnight. With wages indexed to the consumer price index for agricultural labour (CPI-AL), the average wage under the scheme is increased from time-to-

time, resulting in improvement in the bargaining power of agriculture labour. It has also led to improved economic outcomes, especially in watershed activities, and reduction in distress migration.

5.6.7 Work Site Facilities: Work site facilities such as crèche, drinking water, shade have to be provided.

5.6.8 Labour-intensive Works: A 60:40 wage and material ratio has to be maintained. Contractors and use of labour displacing machinery is prohibited.

5.6.9 Permissible Works:

1. Water conservation.
2. Drought proofing (including plantation and afforestation).
3. Irrigation canals.
4. Minor irrigation, horticulture and land development on the lands of scheduled castes, scheduled tribes, and land reform beneficiaries.
5. Renovation of traditional water bodies.
6. Flood protection.
7. Land development.
8. Rural connectivity.
9. Any other work that may be notified by the Central Government in consultation with the State Government.

5.6.10 *Rozgar Jagaran Puruskar*: The objective of the award is to acknowledge the outstanding and exemplary contribution made by a registered civil society organization (CSO) in the effective implementation of the MGNREGS at state, district, block and gram panchayat levels. The award includes a medal, scroll and cash (gram panchayat, ₹ 1,000; intermediate panchayat, ₹ 2,000; district panchayat, ₹ 5,000 and State level, ₹ 25,000).

5.7 National Rural Employment Guarantee Act Software Package (NREGASoft)

In October 2005, Ministry of Rural Development (MoRD) and National Informatics Centre (NIC) commenced the preparation of appropriate e-governance solution to strengthen

MGNREGS and when the scheme was launched in February 2006, the NREGASoft was also launched across the country. The software is available to all stakeholders online through http://nrega.nic.in and also could be downloaded for off-line working. The package is Unicode-enabled and supports local languages. The training to use the software has been organized in States.

NREGAsoft is web-based software prepared to capture all the activities under MGNREGS at national, state, district, block and *panchayat* level. Using this portal each stakeholder can input information and access his/her own information through this portal. NREGAsoft captures registration of workers, work demanded, number of days of employment for whole family, funds transferred/utilized and number of works undertaken under the scheme. Various stake holders of the project are the following:

1. Citizens.
2. *Gram panchayats*, block *panchayats* and *zilla panchayats*.
3. Workers.
4. Programme officers.
5. District programme co-ordinators.
6. Implementing agencies other then *panchayati raj* institutions (PRIs).
7. State rural development departments.
8. Ministry of Rural Development (MoRD) Government of India.

Various modules of the software are the following:

5.7.1 Beneficiary Management Module: It captures registration, demand for work, work allocation and muster rolls on which a person worked. The software has the provision of payment of wages through bank/post office as it captures the bank/post office account number, bank/post office name, branch name for all the persons who demanded job and their account number are shown in muster roll against their name. It also keeps tracks of number of days of employment of a family.

5.7.2 Fund Management Module: It captures the funds transferred from MoRD/States to districts and then to programme officers/panchayats and expenditure incurred by various implementing agencies on labour, material and contingency. Hence, it keeps track of each and every rupee spent under the scheme.

5.7.3 Works Management Module: It captures information about the various works undertaken under the scheme at various levels. It facilitates online approval of projects and keeps track of time taken for approval of project. Each project is provided a unique ID and status of work is maintained in the system.

5.7.4 Grievance Redressal System: It allows a worker/citizen to lodge complaint and trace the subsequent response.

5.7.5 Staffing Position Module: It captures name, telephone numbers etc. of all the officials, planning and implementing agencies from *gram panchayat* to MoRD involved in MGNREGS, thus strengthening communication and coordination among them

5.7.6 Alerts: The software also gives alerts to implementing agencies about the various irregularities, important activities, messages for funds to be received by the agencies.

5.7.7 *Gram Panchayat* Accounting System: MGNREGS puts lot of responsibility on *gram panchayats* as registration, demand for work and allocation of work can be done only by *gram panchayats*. Software assists *gram panchayats* as follows:

1. It keeps track of 100 days of the employment to a family.
2. It ensures that a worker should not work on two worksites simultaneously.
3. It keeps track of the fund released from the MoRD/States to the districts and then from districts to blocks/*gram panchayats*. Thus, it helps in reconciliation of accounts
4. It provides status of available funds in the accounts at panchayats, blocks and districts levels.

5.8 Direct Benefit Transfer (DBT)

In the first decade of its existence, MGNREGS was saddled with several inefficiencies, including widespread corruption, political interference, leakage, and significant delay in wage payments. The programme was reviewed in 2015 and the government initiated major reforms using technology and emphasised on bringing in more transparency and accountability, robust planning and creation of durable productive assets. The scheme was also integrated with the Aadhaar Linked Payments (ALP) system. The ALP leveraged the Jan Dhan, Aadhaar and Mobile (JAM) trinity to provide direct benefit transfers (DBT) to the beneficiaries' bank accounts. As a result, the wage payment system underlying MGNREGS was streamlined, thereby reducing the scope for delays in payment.

Before the implementation of DBT, MGNREGS wages were transferred to the panchayat bank accounts and a significant number of workers had to collect wages in cash from the gram panchayat office. Though attempts were made to implement a system of DBT, two structural constraints limited these attempts. Until 2015, close to 50 percent of the country's population did not have bank accounts. The proportion of unbanked population was significantly higher for rural people who were the target group for MGNREGS. In rural India, banking penetration was extremely low. Second, verifying the identity of genuine beneficiaries and transferring wages directly into their bank accounts posed problems. Various Government initiatives in recent years have facilitated overcoming these structural constraints. Linking the Aadhaar Number to an active bank account was the key to implementing income transfers.

In 2015, the Pradhan Mantri Jan Dhan Yojana (PMJDY) was launched to ensure universal access to banking facilities with at least one basic banking account for every household. PMJDY addressed the issue of banking the unbanked population in the country and Aadhaar provided a credible identity source to whoever wanted to open a bank account. The bank accounts of people, including those opened under PMJDY, were linked to their unique Aadhaar numbers, which facilitated cross verification of identities. By expanding the mobile payment options, the Government was able to ease the connectivity issue as people could get access to banking facilities using their mobile phones. So, the JAM trinity enabled the roll-out of DBT by streamlining the validation/verification of beneficiaries as well as the process for release of funds. This ensured timely transfer of funds to the right beneficiary and enabled effective targeting under welfare schemes.

DBT-enabled MGNREGS has indeed helped to alleviate distress of workers. Post-DBT, delays in the payment of wages has reduced significantly thereby providing livelihood security to people in distress. Both demand and supply of work under MGNREGS has increased, especially in districts suffering from distress. The increase in the number of filled muster rolls also implies that distressed workers indeed turn up more frequently for work. The importance of ALP-enabled MGNREGS in alleviating distress is particularly pronounced for the vulnerable sections of society, including women, persons with disability, scheduled castes (SCs) and scheduled tribes (STs).

DBT focuses on directly transferring funds into the beneficiary bank account. The NREGASoft monitors generation of payment of wages within 15 days. Sustained efforts and intensive engagement with all stakeholders has enabled vast improvements in the timely payment of wages.

DBT has streamlined the fund flow process and helped in better targeting, reduction in delay in payments to beneficiaries, minimizing leakages and above all saving of funds.

Muster rolls are a form of an attendance register. Higher number of filled muster rolls represent higher worker turnout on site. Filled muster rolls have shown a significant increase after implementation of DBT indicating that more people are reporting for work.

Total person days and total person days of vulnerable sections (women, SCs and STs) is also higher in the post-DBT years as compared to pre-DBT years indicating that employment generated is higher post-implementation of DBT. It is also heartening to note that more than 90 percent of the person days benefit the vulnerable sections.

5.8.1 Benefits of DBT: DBT has the following benefits:

1. Providing timely release of payments.
2. Ensuring correct funds are transferred to correct beneficiaries, reducing corruption and leakages in system.
3. Reducing delays and instilling trust and confidence in the system by beneficiaries.
4. Focusing strongly on security, tracking and monitoring of funds (through the use of digital signs/signatures and convergence/interoperability).
5. Reconciliation process during payments between intermediate agencies involved in funds transfer (near real time tracking, accountability and transparency).
6. Streamlining verification process and end-to-end funds release process in all the beneficiary-oriented schemes.

5.9 Aadhar Linked Payments (ALP)

In 2015, the Government introduced ALP in MGNREGS in 300 districts that had a high banking penetration. Remaining districts were covered under ALP in 2016. Conceptually, ALP could speed up the wage payment cycle in the following two ways. First, due to stringent biometric requirements, an Aadhaar linked account is unlikely to belong to a *ghost* beneficiary. Hence, Government officials require less time to verify and audit claims from such accounts. Second, the Central Government, which ultimately foots the bill for the scheme, can transfer wages directly to the bank accounts of the beneficiaries, thereby cutting the bureaucratic red tape.

Given that there has been an increase in amount disbursed to bank accounts post-implementation of ALP and a decline in delayed payments, it is expected that there will be an increase in demand for work under the scheme in distressed areas.

It appears, therefore, that before the implementation of ALP, the rural poor treated MGNREGS as an option to earn additional income during good times rather than a shock absorber during bad times. This actually defeated the purpose of the scheme. Post-implementation of ALP, there is a reversal of trend, wherein an increase in demand for work under MGNREGS is observed in drought affected areas. The change post-ALP implementation suggests that reduction in the delay of payments has an immediate positive effect on the demand for work in distressed times.

5.10 National Electronic Fund Management System (NeFMS)

In order to streamline the system of fund flow and to ensure timely payment of wages, NeFMS was implemented in the year 2016. Under the system, the Central Government directly credits the wages of the MGNREGS workers, on a real time basis, to a specific bank account opened by the State Governments. All the programme officers debit this state-level single account for authorization of wage payment. Currently, NeFMS is implemented in 24 States and 1 Union Territory wherein payment of wages is being credited directly to the bank/post office accounts of MGNREGS workers by the Central Government.

5.11 GeoMGNREGA

GeoMGNREGA uses space technology to develop a database of assets created under MGNREGS using technological interventions like mobile based photo geo-tagging and a GIS based information system for online recording and monitoring. The entire data is in public domain and ensures transparency and public disclosure.

5.12 Recommendations of NCEUS to Improve MGNREGS

National Commission for Enterprises in the Unorganised Sector (NCEUS) in its final report entitled *Challenge of*

Employment in India: An Informal Economy Perspective, submitted in April 2009, reviewed the working of MGNREGS and made a number of recommendations to improve its functioning. Some important recommendations were as under:

1. Limit to employment days under MGNREGS be expanded. The cap of 100 days of employment should be removed in districts where 50 percent of the working population belong to scheduled castes and scheduled tribes.
2. Employment guarantee should be made applicable for each individual rather than per household.
3. MGNREGS activities should be taken up in class B and C municipalities as that would enhance employment opportunities in semi-urban localities.
4. The scheme guidelines should make provision for upgradation of skills of women and men workers so that they are able to take up skilled jobs in the implementation apparatus of the programme.
5. To strengthen the administrative and operational efficiency, the administrative expenditure limits of MGNREGS funds be enhanced to 6 percent.
6. Awareness generation about MGNREGS should be a key component so as to increase the number of beneficiaries and to make the scheme more transparent.
7. Steps should be taken to provide opportunities for *light work* at every worksite for persons who are unable to meet the standard productivity norms due to old age, disability, illness, pregnancy and related conditions.
8. Proactive measures by the State Governments for fulfilling the mandate of 33 percent norm of women's share of MGNREGS.

5.13 New Guidelines to Strengthen MGNREGS

1. *Gram panchayat* or programme officer, as the case may be, shall be bound to accept valid applications and to issue a dated receipt to the applicant.

2. Refusal to accept applications and provide dated receipts will be treated as a contravention under Section 25 of MGNREGA.
3. The provision for submitting applications for work must be kept available on a continuous basis through multiple channels so designated by gram panchayats who may empower ward members, anganwadi workers, school teachers, self-help groups, village-level revenue functionaries, common service centres and MGNREGS Labour Groups to receive applications for work and issue dated receipts on their behalf.
4. Provision must also be made (wherever feasible) for workers to register applications for work through mobile telephones in addition to the MGNREGS website and this should feed in directly into the MIS. In case of mobile telephones, the system must be made convenient to illiterate workers and may include Interactive Voice Response System (IVRS) and voice-enabled interactions. This option must automatically issue dated receipts.
5. State Governments will ensure that the MGNREGS MIS will record the demand for work. It will track (for each GP) the gap between date of application for work and date of opening of work.
6. MGNREGS software will automatically generate the pay order for payment of unemployment allowance to such wage seekers whose demand for work is not met within 15 days of demand. Reports prepared on this will have to be part of the essential set of reports to be tracked at the State level. (Source: Government of India, Ministry of Rural Development, Mihir Shah Committee (2012), *MGNREGA Operational Guidelines*.

5.14 Some Recent Initiatives under MGNREGS

1. **Annual Master Circular:** A master circular was issued in 2016, which consolidated 1039 advisories that had been issued since the inception of the scheme. This master

circular is amended and issued every year. This has helped to streamline the implementation of the scheme and bringing in clarity.

2. **Modifying Wage and Material Ratio:** Durable and productive assets are essential for the sustainable livelihood of the poor people in rural areas. The 60:40 wage and material ratio was mandated at *gram panchayat* level. This often leads to non-productive assets being created simply because 60 percent has to be spent on unskilled wage in a *gram panchayat*. To address this without diluting 60:40 principles, the wage and material ratio of 60:40 was allowed at the district level rather *gram panchayat* level.
3. **Emphasis on Individual Beneficiary Schemes:** A large number of Individual Beneficiary Schemes (IBS) like goat sheds, dairy sheds, wells, farm ponds, vermi-compost pits, water soak pits etc have been taken up in recent years. The emphasis on IBS has resulted in enhanced incomes of the beneficiaries and also improved the quality of assets as the beneficiaries often put in their savings to supplement the contribution of MGNREGS.
4. **Mission Water Conservation (MWC):** Planned and systematic development of land to improve its productivity and harnessing of water through development of watersheds have become the central focus of MGNREGS work across the country.
5. **Support for Drought Proofing:** In 2015-16, provision of additional employment of 50 days in drought affected areas over and above 100 days per household under MGNREGS was approved. The major drought proofing works undertaken under MGNREGS are plantations, afforestation, land development, check dams, wells, trenches, bunds and ponds, percolation tanks.
6. **Increased Accountability:** Various citizen centric mobile Apps like Gram Samvaad Mobile App and JanMnREGA (an asset tracking and feedback app for MGNREGS

assets) have been developed, which aim to empower the rural citizens by providing direct access to information and improve accountability to the people.

7. **Other Initiatives:**

- Inter-departmental convergence and collaboration activities like construction of individual household latrines under the Nirmal Bharat Abhiyan (NBA), construction of anganwadi centres under the Integrated Child Development Services (ICDS) Scheme, construction of village playfields under the Panchayat Yuva Krida aur Khel Abhiyan, and convergence with watershed management programmes.
- Steps to open individual bank/post office accounts for all women workers.
- Identifying and providing job cards to widowed, deserted, and destitute women.
- Initiatives for the disabled and other vulnerable persons by fixing schedule of rates (SoR) based on work and time motion study at state level.
- Adding new works to the existing list of permissible works specifically focused on rural livelihood and agricultural activities.

5.15 MGNREGS in Aatmanirbhar Bharat Abhiyan

On May 12, 2020, Prime Minister Narendra Modi announced the Aatmanirbhar Bharat Abhiyan (Self-reliant India Initiative) which combined relief, policy reforms and fiscal and monetary measures to help companies and individuals to cope with the situation created by Covid-19 pandemic. A mega package of ₹ 20 lakh crore (10 percent of GDP) was announced for the purpose.

The details of the ₹ 20 lakh crore package were announced by Finance Minister Nirmala Sitharaman in five tranches during the next five consecutive days. All the measures were aimed at spurring investment and buffering the economy against the Covid-19 shock.

On May 17, 2020, the Finance Minister announced the

fifth and the final tranche of Aatmanirbhar Bharat Abhiyan. The main focus was on Mahatma Gandhi National Rural Employment Guarantee Scheme (MGNREGS)—the flagship rural job guarantee scheme of the Central Government. In the budget for 2020-21, an allocation of ₹ 61,000 crore was made for the scheme. With millions of daily wagers and others returning to their villages in the wake of Covid-19 pandemic, there was a surge in demand for work in rural areas. Hence, Government announced, as part of the fifth tranche, an additional allocation of ₹ 40,000 crore for MGNREGS. Original allocation and additional allocation made for ₹ 1,01,000 crore, making MGNREGS the only social welfare programme in the country with a kitty of ₹ 1,00,000 crore or more. MGNAREGS has emerged as the backbone of rural income for the poor. It guarantees 100 days of work for one person in a year. The wage rate is ₹ 202 per day. There are demands to increase this limit to 150 days.

5.16 MGNREGS: Concluding Observations

Enactment of MGNREGA was a historic step in the Indian context.

MGNREGS is visualized as a first step towards the realization of the economic right to work as envisioned in the Directive Principles of State Policy in the Constitution of India. It recognizes Article 39 of the Constitution, according to which the State must ensure that "citizens, men and women equally, have the right to an adequate means to livelihood" and Article 41 whereby "the State, shall within the limits of its economic capacity and development, make effective provision for securing Right to Work…".

The potential of the MGNREGS to lead the economy towards a labour-intensive growth path needs to be emphasized in this context. The wage-work programme needs to be seen in a long-term perspective, with a strong planning component, dovetailing it with the ongoing development efforts, incorporating decentralised planning and implementation, skill training, maintenance of public assets and eventually absorbing wage-earners into mainstream employment. The path towards full employment lies in strengthening the sectors where the poor are located and stabilizing their incomes, improving their asset base, constructing basic socio-economic infrastructure at the local level, enabling access to paid work opportunities and exerting an upward pressure on market wages. MGNREGS is expected to create conditions for realisation of the above outcomes.

According to some recent studies, the performance of MGNREGA varies significantly across the States. There are some States where MGNREGS has managed to achieve its key outcomes very well and which have indeed innovated in many respects. In others, performance has been unimpressive and lacklustre. Given that the overall framework for MGNREGS is similar across the States, the variations in performance depend on factors such as political and administrative will of the governments, historical background of the state as well as the nature of civil society and public actions around MGNREGS.

State Governments have the responsibility of framing the rules as well as overseeing the actual implementation of the scheme on the ground. There is a lot of scope for State Governments to innovate and adapt the scheme according to the local requirements. State-specific experiences are important sources for innovations which, in turn, provide valuable lessons for replication. The relative success of the scheme in some regions, and failure in others highlights the need to properly understand the reasons for inter- and intra-state variations and to replicate and adopt features of implementation of the better performing states.

In a number of states, low participation of women in the programme is not due to the lack of demand from women but to the social norms that restrict work participation outside the home. Thus, there are still several hurdles in most of the states for enhancing women's participation in the programme. One of the stated objectives of MGNREGS is to foster a sense of gender equality and encourage women's participation in the economic domain. However, such exclusion only leads to reinforcement of the existing social biases against women and goes against the spirit of MGNREGS. Fostering gender equality also implies that the state must step in to lighten the women's role in the *care economy*.

Overall, even within the existing framework and limitations, many of the problems can be substantially overcome if the political and administrative leadership at the state and local levels plays a more proactive role in implementing the objectives of the MGNREGS.

Several violations of the basic entitlements of workers under the scheme are routinely reported. At the same time, these entitlements become more difficult to safeguard due to low levels of awareness among the workers in several parts of the country. Violations of MGNREGS norms are with respect to issues such as setting up of proper work application process and receipt of applications, payment of minimum wages, delays in payments, and lack of basic facilities at work places. While some of the violations occur due to procedural lapses like over-exacting or non-transparent schedule of rates, defective measurements, and weaknesses in the implementation system, there are also instances of wilful denial of entitlements by the officials.

With a people-centred, demand-driven architecture, completely different from the earlier rural employment programmes, MGNREGS has successfully raised the negotiating power of agricultural labour, resulting in higher agricultural wages, improved economic outcomes leading to reduction in distress migration.

It is important that the selection of works reflects the needs, aspirations and priorities of the local people, without which the community will not necessarily have a sense of ownership of the project. The latter is a vital component of the concept of rural infrastructure creation. The training of a pool of local youth in technical skills must also incorporate their ability to act as social mobilizers.

In short, MGNREGS aims at providing not less than 100

days of guaranteed wage employment in a financial year to every rural household, with a stipulation of one-third participation of women, through creation of assets that address causes of chronic poverty like drought, deforestation, and soil erosion, thus encouraging sustainable development.

For the rural poor, even slightest economic distress can be a threat to their livelihood. The scheme was, therefore, designed such that rural poor could turn to it in times of need and that it could mitigate distress by providing adequate work in times of distress.

6

Food and Nutritional Security

At the time of Independence, the country faced two major nutritional problems; one was the threat of famine and acute starvation due to low agricultural production and lack of appropriate food distribution system. The other was chronic energy deficiency due to poverty, low-literacy, poor access to safe-drinking water, sanitation and health care; these factors led to wide spread prevalence of infections and ill health in children and adults.

During the last 73 years, considerable progress has been achieved. Famines no longer stalk the country. There has been substantial reduction in moderate and severe under-nutrition in children and some improvement in nutritional status of all segments of population. In view of the fact that population growth in India will continue for the next few decades, it is essential that appropriate strategies are devised to improve food and nutrition security of families.

Although the country has been able to eliminate nutritional deficiency syndrome like pellagra, beriberi, scurvy etc. yet chronic energy deficiency among adults, under-nutrition among children and micronutrient deficiencies are still prevalent across all section of the population. The country has adopted a multi-sectoral and multi-pronged strategy to combat these problems and to improve the nutritional status of the population. One half of the children under the age of 5 years in India are moderately or severely malnourished, 30 percent of newborn children are significantly under weight and nearly 60 percent of women are anaemic. National Nutrition Monitoring Bureau (NNMB) Report of December 2006 revealed that the consumption of protective foods such as pulses, green leafy vegetables, milk and fruits was grossly inadequate.

Consequently, the intakes of micronutrients such as iron, vitamin A, riboflavin and folic acid were far below the recommended levels in all the age groups.

6.1 India's Food Security Policy

Food security is one of the major components of social security. It consists of ensuring that food is available at all times, that all persons have means of and access to it, that it is nutritionally adequate in terms of quantity, quality and variety, and that it is acceptable within the given culture. There are three elements in this definition, availability, access and suitability. In recent years, nutrition has been considered as part of food security.

Public distribution system (PDS) is the cornerstone of Government's price policy and food security system in India. It ensures availability of certain essential commodities (sugar, kerosene, rice and wheat) at affordable prices, especially for the poor. Through its agency the Food Corporation of India (FCI), Government procures and stocks foodgrains, which are released every month for distribution through the PDS network across the country. These commodities are distributed to the public through a network of fair price shops (FPS). In addition to this, the system of procurement is also used by the Government to provide minimum support prices to the farmers in order to stabilise agricultural output and income.

India's food security policy was crafted with an aim to attain food self-sufficiency by making basic foodgrains available to all its citizens at affordable prices. To make this possible and to oversee its implementation, the Food Corporation of India (FCI) was set up under the Food Corporations Act, 1964. The FCI procures foodgrains from farmers at the Government declared minimum support price (MSP), stocks them in its warehouses, and then makes them available at affordable rates to the people through the public distribution system (PDS). PDS was restructured into the targeted public distribution system (TPDS) in 1997, under which issue price is different for those above and below the poverty line.

Besides the TPDS, the Government has implemented numerous other programmes aimed at food security, which include: (a) Integrated Child Development Scheme (ICDS) for providing nutrition and healthcare services to children and pregnant women, (b) Antyodaya Anna Yojana for providing affordable food to Below Poverty Level (BPL) households, and (c) Midday Meal Scheme for school children.

At the same time, the Government has been suppressing market prices through extensive restrictions and pricing controls on the free trade in foodgrains, and by providing input subsidies to farmers on water, power and fertilizers.

Over the years, India has successfully transformed itself from a foodgrains importing country to a food self-sufficient country with adequate buffer stocks to see itself through a year or two of bad agriculture.

Through a vast network of PDS outlets across the country, Government tries to deliver some minimal supplies of heavily subsidized foodgrains to below poverty line (BPL) households and also some above poverty line (APL) households. The PDS stores are first given subsidized foodgrains and then instructed to deliver them at below market price to specified households. At times, some unscrupulous storekeepers sell off subsidized foodgrains in the open market, and then adulterate the remaining foodgrains and sell the diluted product to BPL and APL households, who have no choice in the matter.

6.2 National Food Security Act, 2013

Indian National Food Security Act, 2013 (also called Right to Food Act), was signed into law on September 12, 2013. This law aims to provide subsidized foodgrains to poor in India.

Food security means availability of sufficient foodgrains to meet the domestic demand as well as access, at the individual level, to adequate quantities of food at affordable prices. The Act marked a paradigm shift in addressing the problem of food security—from the current welfare approach to a right-based approach. About two-thirds of the population will be entitled to receive subsidized foodgrains under Targeted Public Distribution System—India's principal domestic food aid programme

The Act has been termed as biggest ever experiment in the world for distributing highly subsidized food by any government through a rights-based approach.

Under the provisions of the Act, beneficiaries are entitled to purchase 5 kilograms per eligible person per month of cereals at the following prices: Rice at ₹ 3 per kilogram, wheat at ₹ 2 per kilogram and coarse grains (millet) at ₹ 1 per kilogram. Pregnant women, lactating mothers, and certain categories of children are eligible for daily free meals. The Act provides for penalty for non-compliance by public servants.

6.2.1 Salient Features of the Act: These are as under:

1. 75 percent of rural and 50 percent of the urban population are entitled for 3 years (from enactment) to 5 kilograms of foodgrains per month at ₹ 3, ₹ 2, and ₹ 1 per kilogram for rice, wheat and coarse grains (millet), respectively.
2. The work of identification of eligible households has been left to the State Governments.
3. Pregnant women and lactating mothers are entitled to a nutritious *take home ration* of 600 calories and a maternity benefit of at least ₹ 6,000 for 6 months;
4. Children 6 months to 14 years of age are to receive free hot meals [1] or *take home rations.*
5. Central Government will provide funds to State Governments in case of short supplies of foodgrains.
6. Current foodgrains allocation of the States will be protected by the Central Government for at least 6 months.
7. State Governments will provide a food security allowance to the beneficiaries in case of non-supply of foodgrains.
8. Public distribution system (PDS) is to be reformed.
9. Eldest woman in the household, 18 years or above, will be the head of the household for the issuance of the ration card.

10. There will be state- and district-level redress mechanisms.
11. State Food Commissions will be formed for implementation and monitoring of the provisions of the Act.

6.2.2 Main Provisions of the Act: These are as under:

A. Preliminaries: The Act extends to the whole of India and "shall be deemed to have come into force on the 5th day of July 2013" (this is the date when the National Food Security Ordinance 2013 came into force).

B. Entitlements:

(a) Public Distribution System (PDS)*:* Priority households are entitled to 5 kilograms of foodgrains per person per month, and Antyodaya households to 35 kilograms per household per month. The combined coverage of Priority and Antyodaya households (called *eligible households*) shall extend *up to 75 percent of the rural population and up to 50 percent of the urban population*. The PDS issue prices are given in Schedule I: ₹ 3, ₹ 2 and ₹ 1 per kilogram for rice, wheat and millets respectively. These may be revised after 3 years.

(b) Children's Entitlements: These are as shown in Table 6.1.

Table 6.1: Children's Entitlements

For children in the age group of 6 months to 6 years.	An age-appropriate meal, free of charge, through the local anganwadi.
For children aged 6-14 years.	One free mid-day meal every day (except on school holidays) in all government and government-aided schools, up to Class VIII.
For children below six months.	Exclusive breastfeeding shall be promoted.
For children who suffer from malnutrition.	Meals will be provided to them free of charge through the local anganwadi.

(c) Entitlements of Pregnant and Lactating Women: Every pregnant and lactating mother is entitled to a free meal at the local *anganwadi* (during pregnancy and 6 months after child birth) as well as maternity benefits of ₹ 6,000, in instalments.

The entitlements of women and children are to be delivered by State Governments through schemes in accordance with guidelines to be prescribed by the Central Government.

C. Identification of Eligible Households: The Act does not specify criteria for the identification of households eligible for PDS entitlements. The Central Government is to determine the state-wise coverage of the PDS (proportion of the rural/urban population). Then number of eligible persons will be calculated from Census population figures. The identification of eligible households is left to State Governments, subject to the scheme's guidelines for Antyodaya, and subject to guidelines to be specified by the State Government for Priority households. The identification of eligible households is to be completed within 365 days. The lists of eligible households are to be placed in the public domain and "displayed prominently".

D. State Food Commissions: The Act provides for the creation of State Food Commissions. The main function of a State Food Commission will be: (a) to monitor the implementation of the Act, (b) give advice to the State Government and its agencies and (c) inquire into violations of entitlements.

State Food Commissions will also hear appeals against orders of the District Grievance Redressal Officer and prepare annual reports.

E. Transparency and Grievance Redressal: The Act provides for a two-tier grievance redressal structure, involving the District Grievance Redressal Officer (DGRO) and State Food Commission. State Governments must also put in place an internal grievance redressal mechanism which may include call centres, helplines etc.

(a) Transparency Provisions: Mandatory transparency

provisions include the following:

1. Placing all PDS-related records in the public domain.
2. Conducting periodic social audits of the PDS and other welfare schemes.
3. Using information and communication technology to ensure transparent recording of transactions at all levels.
4. Setting up vigilance committees at all levels to supervise all schemes under the Act.

(b) District Grievance Redressal Officers (DGROs): DGROs shall be appointed by State Governments for each district to hear complaints and take necessary action according to norms to be prescribed by State Governments. If a complainant is not satisfied, he or she may file an appeal before the State Food Commission.

(c) Penalties and Compensation: A State Food Commission has powers to impose penalties. If an order of the DGRO is not complied with, the concerned authority or officer can be fined up to ₹ 5,000. The Commission can authorise any of its members to act as an adjudicating officer for this purpose. In case of non-supply of the entitled quantities of foodgrains or meals to entitled persons, such persons will be entitled to a food security allowance from the State Government, as prescribed by the Central Government.

F. Other Provisions: These are as under:

(a) PDS Reforms: In Chapter V, the Act states that Central and State Governments "shall endeavour to progressively undertake" various PDS reforms, including the following:

1. Doorstep delivery of foodgrains.
2. End-to-end computerization.
3. Leveraging "aadhaar" (UID) for unique identification of entitled beneficiaries.
4. Full transparency of records.
5. Preference to public institutions or bodies in licensing of fair price shops.
6. Management of fair price shops by women or their collectives.

7. Diversification of commodities distributed under the PDS.
8. Introduction of schemes such as cash transfer, food coupons or other schemes to the targeted beneficiaries in order to ensure their foodgrains entitlements as prescribed by the Central Government.

(b) Obligations of Government and Local Authorities: The main obligation of the Central Government is to provide foodgrains (or, failing that, funds) to State Governments, at prices specified in Schedule I, to implement the main entitlements. The Central Government has wide-ranging powers to make Rules in consultation with the State Governments.

The main obligation of State Governments is to implement the relevant schemes, in accordance with the Central Government guidelines. State Governments also have wide-ranging powers to make Rules. They are free to extend benefits and entitlements beyond what is prescribed in the Act, from their own resources.

Local authorities and panchayati raj institutions are responsible for proper implementation of the Act in their respective areas, and may be given additional responsibilities by notification.

G. Schedules: The Act has the following four schedules (which can be amended by notification).

1. Schedule I prescribes issue prices for the PDS.
2. Schedule II prescribes nutritional standards for mid-day meals, take-home rations and related entitlements.
3. Schedule III lists various provisions for advancing food security.
4. Schedule IV specifies a minimum foodgrains allocation for each state, in the case of states that might lose otherwise under the Act. This essentially means continuing of existing allocations.

6.2.3 Critical Assessment: For proponents, food security is a form of investment in human capital. It will bring some security in people's lives and make it easier for them to meet their basic needs, protect their health, educate their children, and take risks.

Criticism of the Act includes accusations of both political motivation and fiscal irresponsibility. According to some, food prices are still elevated and the food security Act will aggravate food price inflation as it will tilt supply towards cereals and away from other farm produce (proteins), which will raise food prices further. It is also feared that the legislation would: (a) restrict private initiative in agriculture, (b) reduce competition in the marketplace due to government domination of the grain market, (c) shift money from investments in agriculture to subsidies and (d) continue focus on cereals production when shifts in consumer demand patterns indicate a need to focus more on protein, fruits and vegetables.

6.3 Forests and Food Security

Food security is the outcome of complex interactions among natural resource management, political, social, and economic factors. Forests, as an important element within this matrix, affect food security in three major areas:

6.3.1 Forests and Agriculture: Forests help maintain favourable and stable conditions needed for sustained agricultural productivity. Moisture and nutrient leaching from the adjoining forests maintain the fertility of the agriculture fields. It is common in forest regions of Eastern India plateau (Northern Odisha, Jharkhand, and Eastern Chhattisgarh) for farmers to desist from the use of chemical fertilizers. Thus, many farmers leave their fields near a moderately dense forest to be fed entirely from moisture and nutrient from the forests and save the precious cow dung to fertilize more distant fields.

Over the years, local communities have developed sophisticated indigenous techniques to augment and harvest forest-based moisture and nutrient flow. Raised bunds on forest boundaries along the contours are common in the Eastern India plateau. Further, in recent years a cash rich economy has developed in many forest areas when farmers found out that fields at the foot of the forested hills are best suited for potato cultivation, as these have accumulated rich potash deposit that has leached down from the uphill forests.

Windbreaks and shelterbelts protect crops from drying and damaging winds. Local people fully appreciate the importance of forests in disease control and prevention of epidemic outbreak related to agriculture crops. Local villagers in forested regions appreciate the role of avifauna in the control of rodent and insect pests. Forests also serve as the chief source of tree fodder for feeding livestock. Of growing importance is the role forests play as storehouses of biodiversity, potentially very important in future crop breeding and pest and disease management programmes.

6.3.2 Forest Foods: Forest foods are important for the local villagers during both stress and normal periods, and the use of forest foods as a component of local response strategies to increasing food insecurity is widely documented. In normal times, leafy vegetables, mushroom, berries and fruits available in different seasons form the usual component of their diet. Having a diverse resource base with a range of different trees, plants and insect species, forests increase the options for maintaining food security. Different seasonal products complement each other with seasonally different pattern of availability. Leafy vegetables and fruits provide essential vitamins and minerals as dietary supplements. Similarly, wild fruits are very rich in Vitamin A and C.

Moreover, the forest foods have a definite pro-poor bias. Women and children are the largest consumers, followed by the elderly. In the wake of social customs forcing rural women to eat at the end—and at times only the left over and poor portions of the cooked meal—such harvests do help women regain some nutrition. During the periods of acute food shortage, forest foods sustain livelihoods.

6.3.3 Forests and Fisheries: Forests also have significant links with inland and marine fisheries. Rivers and streams are rich fishing grounds for local populations. Forests regulate the volume and fluctuations of stream flows and provide a shaded riparian environment favourable for the development of smaller life forms which fish feed on. Villagers in the forest region of Eastern India plateau know that the water flowing from bamboo forests has high nutrient capacity and is able to support larger volumes and healthy population of edible aquatic fauna (fish, crab, mussel, snail etc.).

The mangrove swamps in southern India provide habitats for many fish species, especially shrimps. The fish catch from these areas not only enriches protein-deficient diets and generates household income, but also helps maintain/enrich local level social capital when the whole village gathers to celebrate community fish harvesting festivals based on the principles of strict equality in sharing of the catch.

To sum up, pioneering work by agriculture scientists and the efforts of farmers had helped achieve a breakthrough in the agriculture sector in the 1960s, popularly known as the *Green Revolution*. High agricultural production and productivity achieved in subsequent years has been the main reason for attaining food security to a large extent. The country has not witnessed any big technological breakthrough in agriculture since then. The food safety net for each and every citizen requires enhanced agricultural production and productivity in the form of a Second Green Revolution.

Further, special attention is required for achieving higher production and productivity levels in pulses, oilseeds, fruits, and vegetables, which had remained untouched in the First Green Revolution but are essential for nutritional security. In this regard, achieving high production of poultry, meat and fisheries is also essential. The relatively weak supply responses to price hikes in agricultural commodities, especially food articles, in the recent past brings back into focus the central question of efficient supply chain management and need for sustained levels of growth in agriculture and allied sectors. The choice before the country is clear—to invest more in agriculture and allied sectors with the right strategies, policies, and interventions. This is also a necessary condition for inclusive growth and for ensuring that the benefits of growth reach a larger number of people.

Food security of India is closely related to development of technologies for increasing the agriculture outputs through process innovations for land saving and water use. The question is how to develop and deploy new agro biotechnology tools and precision agriculture for increasing the output of agriculture sector in the country.

Endnote

1. *Meal* is defined as hot cooked or pre-cooked and heated before its service meal or take home ration, as may be prescribed by the Central Government. All meals have to meet nutritional norms specified in Schedule II of the Act.

7

Three-tier Universal Security System for the Poor

Encouraged by the success of the Pradhan Mantri Jan Dhan Yojana, the Government of India proposed to work towards creating a universal social security system for all Indians, specially the poor and the under-privileged and the workers in the unorganised sector, using the bank accounts as the basis for launching the schemes.

Jan Dhan Yojana ensures universal banking coverage across all the six lakh villages of the country, by providing at least one basic banking account, per household. It provides all households in the country, both rural and urban, access to multiple financial services like bank account with RuPay debit card, access to credit, remittance, insurance and pension. Thus, the mission not only brought the excluded sections from the society into the financial mainstream but made the transfer of benefits of various subsidy schemes of the government more efficient. It was the first step to bring in economic equality and remove financial untouchability.

In order to achieve the goal of universal social security system, especially for the poor and the under-privileged, the three-tier social security schemes, announced in the 2015-16 budget, have spread the safety net of protection to people in all strata of life against deprivation and uncertainties. They are the steps towards ensuring financial security and long-term sustenance to families when the earning family member retires, dies or suffers full or partial disability.

A large portion of India's population had been living without any kind of health, accidental, or life insurance for so long. It was estimated that the unorganised sector workers, which constitute 88 percent of the total labour force of 47.29

crore, as per the 66th Round of NSSO Survey of 2011-12, did not have any formal pension provision. The Budget 2015-16 highlighted this issue and proposed the following three social security schemes:

1. Pradhan Mantri Suraksha Bima Yojna.
2. Pradhan Mantri Jeevan Jyoti Bima Yojana.
3. Atal Pension Yojana.

Prime Minister launched the three social security schemes on May 9, 2015. These three schemes are based on Jan Dhan Yojana platform to protect poor and underprivileged citizens at the time of illness, accidents or old age.

7.1 Pradhan Mantri Suraksha Bima Yojna (PMSBY)

The objective of this scheme is to ensure risk coverage in case of accidental death, full or partial disability. The insured amount for accidental death and full disability is ₹ 2 lakh and it is ₹ 1 lakh for partial disability. It has an annual premium of ₹ 12 only, which will be directly auto-debited by the bank from the subscriber's account. It is the only mode of paying the premium and thus creates a linkage between the beneficiary and the bank. A person has to opt for the scheme every year by submitting a simple form to the bank by June 1. One can also opt for the scheme on a long-term basis and in that case his account will be auto-debited every year by the bank. People between the age of 18 and 70 years, having an Aadhaar-linked bank account, are eligible for the scheme.

The scheme is offered to all Public Sector General Insurance Companies (PSGICs) and other willing insurers who are ready to tie-up with banks for this purpose. It has the provision for Government contribution, by which various Ministries can co-contribute premium for beneficiaries of different categories from their budget or from the Public Welfare Fund, created in the budget 2015-16, out of unclaimed money.

The scheme is a 1 year cover, renewable from year to year, Accident Insurance Scheme offering accidental death and disability cover for death or disability on account of an accident. The scheme would be offered/administered through PSGICs and other general insurance companies willing to offer the product on similar terms with necessary approvals and tie-up with banks for this purpose. Participating banks will be free to engage any such insurance company for implementing the scheme for their subscribers.

7.1.1 Scope of Coverage: All savings bank account holders in the age group 18 to 70 years in participating banks will be entitled to join. In case of multiple saving bank accounts held by an individual in one or different banks, the person would be eligible to join the scheme through one savings bank account only. Aadhaar would be the primary KYC for the bank account.

7.1.2 Enrolment Modality/Period: The cover is for 1 year period stretching from June 1 to May 31 for which option to join/pay by auto-debit from the designated savings bank account on the prescribed forms is required to be given by May 31 of every year. However, applicants may give an indefinite/longer option for enrolment/auto-debit, subject to continuation of the scheme with terms as may be revised on the basis of past experience. Individuals who exit the scheme at any point may re-join the scheme in future years through the above modality. New entrants into the eligible category from year to year or currently eligible individuals who did not join earlier shall be able to join in future years while the scheme is continuing.

7.1.3 Benefits: These are as given in Table 7.1.

7.1.4 Premium: ₹ 12 per annum per member. The premium will be deducted from the account holder's savings bank account through *auto debit* facility in one instalment on or before June 1, of each annual coverage period under the scheme. However, in cases where auto debit takes place after June 1, the cover shall commence from the first day of the month following the auto debit.

The premium would be reviewed based on annual claims experience. However, barring unforeseen adverse outcomes of extreme nature, efforts would be made to ensure that there is no upward revision of premium in the first three years.

7.1.5 Eligibility Conditions: The savings bank account holders of the participating banks aged between 18 years and 70 years who give their consent to join/enable auto-debit, as per the above modality, will be enrolled into the scheme.

Table 7.1: Benefits of Pradhan Mantri Suraksha Bima Yojna

S. No.	Death/disability	Sum insured (₹)
1.	Death	2 lakh
2.	Total and irrecoverable loss of both eyes or loss of use of both hands or feet or loss of sight of one eye and loss of use of hand or foot	2 lakh
3.	Total and irrecoverable loss of sight of one eye or loss of use of one hand or foot	1 lakh

7.1.6 Master Policy Holder: Participating bank will be the master policy holder on behalf of the participating subscribers. A simple and subscriber-friendly administration and claim settlement process shall be finalized by the respective general insurance company in consultation with the participating banks.

7.1.7 Termination of Cover: The accident cover for the member shall terminate on any of the following events and no benefit will be payable there under:

1. On attaining the age of 70 years.
2. Closure of account with the bank or insufficiency of balance to keep the insurance in force.
3. In case a member is covered through more than one account and premium is received by the insurance company inadvertently, insurance cover will be restricted to one only and the premium shall be liable to be forfeited.
4. If the insurance cover is ceased due to any technical reasons such as insufficient balance on due date or due to

any administrative issues, the same can be reinstated on receipt of full annual premium, subject to conditions that may be laid down. During this period, the risk cover will be suspended and reinstatement of risk cover will be at the sole discretion of insurance company.

5. Participating banks will deduct the premium amount in the same month when the auto-debit option is given, preferably in May of every year, and remit the amount due to the Insurance Company in that month itself.

7.1.8 Administration: The scheme, subject to the above, will be administered as per the standard procedure stipulated by the insurance company. The data flow process and data proforma will be provided separately.

It will be the responsibility of the participating bank to recover the appropriate annual premium from the account holders within the prescribed period through *auto-debit* process.

Enrolment form/auto-debit authorization in the prescribed proforma shall be obtained and retained by the participating bank. In case of claim, the insurance company may seek submission of the same. Insurance company reserves the right to call for these documents at any point of time.

The acknowledgement slip may be made into an acknowledgement slip-cum-certificate of insurance.

The experience of the scheme will be monitored on yearly basis for re-calibration etc., as may be necessary.

7.1.9 Appropriation of Premium:

1. Insurance premium to insurance company: ₹ 10 per annum per member
2. Reimbursement of expenses to BC/Micro/Corporate/Agent: ₹ 1 per annum per member.
3. Reimbursement of administrative expenses to participating bank: ₹ 1 per annum per member.

The scheme commenced on June 1, 2015. The next annual renewal date shall be each successive June 1 in subsequent years. The scheme is liable to be discontinued prior to commencement of a new future renewal date if circumstances so require.

7.2 Pradhan Mantri Jeevan Jyoti Bima Yojana (PMJJBY)

This scheme is to benefit people in case of death. It is available to people in the age group of 18 to 50 years, having a bank account. People, who join this scheme before completing the age of 50 years, can continue to have the risk of life cover up to the age of 55 years, subject to the payment of premium. The scheme has an annual premium of ₹ 330, with a risk coverage of ₹ 2 lakh. The premium will be directly auto-debited by the bank from the subscriber's account. It is the only mode of paying the premium and thus creates a linkage between the beneficiary and the bank. It has the provision for Government contribution, by which various Ministries can co-contribute premium for beneficiaries of different categories from their budget or from the Public Welfare Fund, created in the budget 2015-16, out of unclaimed money.

A person can opt for the scheme for a year or prefer to continue it as a long-term option. In case of long-term option, his account will be auto-debited every year by the bank.

Life Insurance Corporation (LIC) and other willing life insurers with a tie-up with the bank are to implement the scheme. The scheme also has the provision for co-contribution of premium by various Ministries for different categories of their beneficiaries out of their budget or out of Public Welfare Fund created in the Budget 2015-16 from the unclaimed money.

The scheme is a 1 year cover, renewable from year to year. It offers life insurance cover for death due to any reason. The scheme is offered/administered through LIC and other life insurance companies willing to offer the product on similar terms with necessary approvals and tie-ups with banks for this purpose. Participating banks will be free to engage any such life insurance company for implementing the scheme for their subscribers.

7.2.1 Scope of Coverage: All savings bank account holders in the age group 18 to 50 years in participating banks will be entitled to join. In case of multiple saving bank accounts held by an individual in one or different banks, the person would be eligible to join the scheme through one savings bank account only. Aadhaar would be the primary KYC for the bank account.

7.2.2 Enrolment Period: Initially on launch for the cover period June 1, 2015 to May 31, 2016, subscribers were required to enrol and give their auto-debit consent by May 31, 2015. Late enrolment for prospective cover was possible up to August 31, 2015. Those joining subsequently may be able to do so with payment of full annual premium for prospective cover, with submission of a self-certificate of good health in the prescribed proforma.

7.2.3 Enrolment Modality: The cover shall be for the 1 year period stretching from June 1 to May 31 for which option to join/pay by auto-debit from the designated savings bank account on the prescribed forms will be required to be given by May 31 of every year, with the exception as above for the initial year. Delayed enrolment with payment of full annual premium for prospective cover may be possible with submission of a self-certificate of good health.

Individuals who exit the scheme at any point may re-join the scheme in future years by submitting a declaration of good health in the prescribed proforma.

In future years, new entrants into the eligible category or currently eligible individuals who did not join earlier or discontinued their subscription shall be able to join while the scheme is continuing, subject to submission of self-certificate of good health.

7.2.4 Benefits: ₹ 2 lakh is payable on member's death due to any reason.

7.2.5 Premium: ₹ 330 per annum per member. The premium will be deducted from the account holder's savings bank account through auto-debit facility in one instalment, as per the option given, on or before May 31 of each annual coverage period under the scheme. Delayed enrolment for prospective cover after May 31 will be possible with full payment of annual premium and submission of a self-certificate of good health. The premium would be reviewed based on annual claims experience. However, barring unforeseen adverse outcomes of extreme nature, efforts would be made to ensure that there is no upward revision of premium in the first three years.

7.2.6 Eligibility Conditions:

1. The savings bank account holders of the participating banks aged between 18 years and 50 years who give their consent to join/enable auto-debit, as per the above modality, will be enrolled into the scheme.
2. Individuals who join after the initial enrolment period extending up to August 31, 2015 or November 30, 2015, as the case may be, will be required to give a self-certification of good health and that he/she does not suffer from any of the critical illnesses as mentioned in the applicable consent-cum-declaration form as on date of enrolment or earlier.

7.2.7 Master Policy Holder: Participating banks will be the master policy holders. A simple and subscriber-friendly administration and claim settlement process shall be finalized by LIC/other insurance companies in consultation with the participating bank.

7.2.8 Termination of Assurance: The assurance on the life of the member shall terminate on any of the following events and no benefit will become payable there under:

1. On attaining age 55 years subject to annual renewal up to that date (entry, however, will not be possible beyond the age of 50 years).
2. Closure of account with the bank or insufficiency of balance to keep the insurance in force.
3. In case a member is covered under PMJJBY with LIC of India/other company through more than one account and premium is received by LIC/other company inadvertently, insurance cover will be restricted to ₹ 2 lakh and the premium shall be liable to be forfeited.
4. If the insurance cover is ceased due to any technical

reasons such as insufficient balance on due date or due to any administrative issues, the same can be reinstated on receipt of full annual premium and a satisfactory statement of good health.

5. Participating banks shall remit the premium to insurance companies in case of regular enrolment on or before June 30 every year and in other cases in the same month when received.

7.2.9 Administration: The scheme, subject to the above, will be administered by the LIC/other insurance company set-ups. The data flow process and data proforma will be informed separately.

It will be the responsibility of the participating bank to recover the appropriate annual premium in one instalment, as per the option, from the account holders on or before the due date through auto-debit process.

Members may also give one-time mandate for auto-debit every year till the scheme is in force.

Enrolment form/auto-debit authorization/consent-cum-declaration form in the prescribed proforma shall be obtained and retained by the participating bank. In case of claim, LIC/insurance company may seek submission of the same. LIC/insurance company reserves the right to call for these documents at any point of time.

The acknowledgement slip may be made into an acknowledgement slip-cum-certificate of insurance.

The experience of the scheme will be monitored on yearly basis for re-calibration etc. as may be necessary.

7.2.10 Appropriation of Premium:

1. Insurance premium to LIC/insurance company: ₹ 289 per annum per member.
2. Reimbursement of expenses to BC/micro/corporate/agent: ₹ 30 per annum per member.
3. Reimbursement of administrative expenses to participating Bank: ₹ 11 per annum per member

The scheme commenced on June 1, 2015. The next annual

renewal date shall be each successive June 1, in subsequent years.

The scheme is liable to be discontinued prior to commencement of a new future renewal date if circumstances so require.

PMSBY and PMJJBY will provide much needed access to affordable personal accident and life cover to a vast population, currently not having convenient and systematic access of this nature. It will go a long way in improving insurance awareness and insurance penetration/density in the country. Jan Dhan to Jan Suraksha ensures financial inclusion and financial security, and all round development of citizens of India.

7.3 Atal Pension Yojana (APY)

The Government of India is extremely concerned about the old age income security of the working poor and is focused on encouraging and enabling them to join the National Pension System (NPS). To address the longevity risks among the workers in unorganised sector and to encourage the workers in unorganised sector to voluntarily save for their retirement, who constitute 88 percent of the total labour force of 47.29 crore as per the 66th Round of NSSO Survey of 2011-12, but do not have any formal pension provision, the Government had started the Swavalamban Scheme in 2010-11. However, coverage under Swavalamban Scheme is inadequate mainly due to lack of guaranteed pension benefits at the age of 60.

Government of India's concern for old age income security for the working poor, particularly in the unorganised sector, resulted in the creation of a new initiative in the budget proposals for 2015-16, called Atal Pension Yojana. It is to encourage the uninsured workers in the unorganised sector to come under the National Pension System (NPS), under the Pension Fund Regulatory and Development Authority (PFRDA).

APY will provide a defined pension, depending on the contribution, and its period. The APY will be focussed on all citizens in the unorganised sector, who join the National Pension System (NPS) administered by the Pension Fund

Regulatory and Development Authority (PFRDA).

1. The individual subscribers shall have an option to make the contribution on a monthly, quarterly, half yearly basis instead of on a monthly basis earlier.
2. Discontinuation of payment of contribution provision has been substantially modified in favour of the subscriber. The account will not be deactivated and closed till the account balance with self-contributions minus the Government co-contributions becomes zero due to deduction of account maintenance charges and fees.
3. Also the penalty on delayed payment has been simplified to ₹ 1 per month for contribution of ₹ 100, or part thereof, for each delayed monthly payment instead of different slabs given earlier.
4. Similarly, premature exit from the scheme before 60 years of age was not permitted earlier except in exceptional circumstances, i.e. in the event of the death of the beneficiary or terminal disease. Now the modified provision permits the subscriber to voluntarily exit with the conditions that: (a) he shall only be refunded the contributions made by him to APY, along with the net actual interest earned on his contributions (after deducting the account maintenance charges) and (b) the Government co-contribution, and the interest earned on the Government co-contribution, shall not be returned to such subscribers.

Under the APY, the subscribers would receive the fixed minimum pension of ₹ 1,000 per month, ₹ 2,000 per month, ₹ 3,000 per month, ₹ 4,000 per month, ₹ 5,000 per month, at the age of 60 years, depending on their contributions, which itself would be based on the age of joining the APY. The minimum age of joining APY is 18 years and maximum age is 40 years. Therefore, minimum period of contribution by any subscriber under APY would be 20 years or more. The benefit of fixed minimum pension would be guaranteed by the Government. The APY was introduced from June 1, 2015.

8

Farmer-friendly Schemes

Agricultural sector occupies a key position in the Indian economy. Agriculture (inclusive of animal husbandry, forestry and fishing) is central to the nutrition needs of India and also remains the largest sector of India's economy as a source of employment.

When countrywide lockdown was announced from March 25, 2020, most of the economic activities came to a grinding halt in urban areas. However, rural India continued to be normal in view of the exemption from restrictions allowed to farmers to conduct farming operations, including harvesting and transporting their produce to grain markets with the general conditions of face covering, hand hygiene and social distancing. These exemptions helped to maintain continuity in supply chain, especially in view of harvesting and sowing season. Food Corporation of India and State Governments carried out massive procurement of *rabi* crops, mainly wheat.

India's foodgrains production was 285 million tonnes (MT) in 2018-19 which rose to record level of 295 MT in 2019-20. The target for 2020-21 has been set at 298 MT.

With industrial and services sectors showing signs of slowdown, a vibrant agricultural sector is a silver lining in the otherwise gloomy scenario. The share of agriculture in gross domestic product (GDP), which has been declining for quite some time and hovers around 14-15 percent, is likely to increase.

8.1 Doubling Farmers Income by 2022-23

While talking about income of the farmers at a Kisan Rally in Bareilly (Uttar Pradesh) on February 28, 2016, the Prime Minister stated that it is his dream to see farmers double their income by 2022, when the country completes 75 years of its

Independence. It is obvious that he was referring to double the current income of the farmers or income for the agricultural year 2015-16 by agricultural year 2022-23, i.e. 7 years away from the base year 2015-16.

Farmers make up nearly half of India's workforce. Therefore, for India to flourish, its farmers and the farm economy must prosper. It is against this background that the Prime Minister has called for doubling farmers' incomes by 2022. To achieve this goal, a strong programme for agricultural transformation is required. It should include numerous measures to raise farm productivity, bring remunerative prices to farmers, put farmers' land to productive uses when they are not able to farm it themselves and improve the implementation of relief measures.

Enhancing agricultural productivity requires efficient use of inputs, introduction of new technologies and shifting from low to high value commodities. It needs to expand the scope of irrigation to increase crop intensity, improve access to irrigation, enhance the seed replacement rate and encourage the balanced use of fertilizers. Precision farming and related new technologies, that allow highly efficient farming and conserve resources, must be spread through appropriate policy interventions. Conditions conducive to shift into high value commodities such as horticulture, dairying, poultry, piggery, small ruminant husbandry, fisheries and forestry need to be created.

Unsurprisingly, the Prime Minister has set the goal of doubling farmers' income by 2022-23 over that in 2015-16. Achieving this goal would require significantly faster growth in nearly all variables that positively impact farmers' incomes.

8.2 Direct Benefit Transfer (DBT) in Fertiliser Sector

The Government of India introduced DBT system for fertilizer subsidy on pilot basis with effect from October 2016. Under the fertilizer DBT system, 100 percent subsidy on various fertilizer grades is released to the fertilizer companies on the basis of actual sales made by the retailers to the beneficiaries. The sale of all subsidized fertilizers to farmers/buyers is made through Point of Sale (PoS) devices installed at each retail shop and the beneficiaries are identified through Aadhaar Card, Kisan Credit Card (KCC), Voter Identity Card etc. The implementation of the DBT scheme requires development of PoS devices at every retail shop, training of retailers for using PoS device, stock initialization in the PoS device after verifying the physical stock at retail point, before making sales transactions. Presently, the DBT scheme is under implementation in 17 pilot districts. Based on the deployment of PoS devices in different States, the Department of Fertilizers will extend the DBT scheme to other States in a phased manner.

As on December 22, 2017, 14 States/Union Territories had been brought under DBT framework. The benefits of the DBT scheme are as under:

1. DBT framework is a beneficiary-driven subsidy payment mechanism at national level.
2. It creates Aadhaar-seeded data base of beneficiaries and provides transaction visibility at the level of buyers.
3. By linking the actual sales to subsidy payments, it facilitates a more transparent and faster tracking of funds along the value chain, i.e. from manufacturers to beneficiaries.
4. Diversion of fertilizers is expected to be minimized.

8.3 Remunerative Minimum Support Prices (MSPs)

An important element of the agricultural price policy of the Government of India is the announcement every year of MSPs for major commodities. The co-operative societies and government agencies have helped the farmers to escape the exploitative practices of the private traders.

Assurance of a remunerative and stable price environment is considered very important for increasing agricultural production and productivity since the market place for agricultural produce tends to be inherently unstable, which often inflicts undue losses on the growers, even when they adopt the best available technology package and produce efficiently. Towards this end, MSPs for major agricultural products are fixed by the Government, each year, after taking into account the cost of inputs.

Policy of the Government regarding MSPs was enunciated by the Finance Minister Arun Jaitley in his budget speech to the Parliament on February 1, 2018. He said, "...in our party's manifesto it has been stated that the farmers should realize at least 50 percent more than the cost of their produce, in other words, one and a half times of the cost of their production. Government has been very much sensitive to this resolutions and it has declared minimum support price (MSP) for the majority of rabi crops at least at one and a half times the cost involved. Now, we have decided to implement this resolution as a principle for the rest of crops". [1]

On June 1, 2020, Central Government announced higher MSPs for 14 kharif (summer sown) crops for 2020-21. The support price for the most popular kharif crop paddy was increased from ₹ 1,815 per quintal to ₹ 1,868 per quintal.

8.4 Pradhan Mantri Fasal Bima Yojana (PMFBY)

Prime Minister Narendra Modi unveiled the new scheme Pradhan Mantri Fasal Bima Yojana (PMFBY) on January 13, 2016. This scheme will help in decreasing the burden of premiums on farmers who take loans for their cultivation and will also safeguard them against the inclement weather.

It has also been decided to make the settlement process of the insurance claim, fast and easy so that the farmers do not face any trouble regarding the crop insurance plan. This scheme will be implemented in every state of India, in association with respective State Governments. The scheme will be administered under the Ministry of Agriculture and Farmers Welfare, Government of India.

8.4.1 Objectives of the Scheme: These are as under:

1. To provide insurance coverage and financial support to the farmers in the event of failure of any of the notified crop as a result of natural calamities, pests and diseases.
2. To stabilize the income of farmers to ensure their continuous process in farming.
3. To encourage farmers to adopt innovative and modern agricultural practices.
4. To ensure flow of credit to the agriculture sector.

8.4.2 Highlight of the Scheme:

1. There will be a uniform premium of only 2 percent to be paid by farmers for all kharif crops and 1.5 percent for all rabi crops. In case of annual commercial and horticultural crops, the premium to be paid will be only 5 percent.
2. The premium rates to be paid by farmers are very low and balance premium will be paid by the Government to provide full insured amount to the farmers against crop loss in any natural calamities.
3. There is no upper limit on Government subsidy. Even if balance premium is 90 percent, it will be borne by the Government.
4. Earlier, there was a provision of capping the premium rate which is low claims being paid to farmers. Now this is removed and farmers will get claim against full sum insured without any reduction.
5. The use of technology will be encouraged to a great extent. Smart phones, remote sensing drone and GPS technologies will be used to capture and upload data of crop cutting to reduce the delays in the claim payment.
6. The insurance plan will be handled under a single insurance company, Agriculture Insurance Company of India (AIC).

PMFBY is a replacement scheme of National Agriculture Insurance Scheme (NAIS) and Modified National Agriculture Insurance Scheme (MNAIS) and hence exempted from the service tax.

Moreover, District Level Monitoring Committee (DLMC)

already overseeing the implementation and monitoring of the ongoing crop insurance schemes like National Agricultural Insurance Scheme (NAIS), Weather Based Crop Insurance Scheme (WBCIS), Modified National Agricultural Insurance Scheme (MNAIS) and Coconut Palm Insurance Scheme (CPIS) shall be responsible for proper management of the Scheme.

Regarding PMFBY, the Finance Minister Arun Jaitley in his 2017-18 Budget Speech on February 1 observed, "At the time of sowing, farmers should feel secure against natural calamities. The *Fasal Bima Yojana* launched by our Government is a major step in this direction. The coverage of this scheme will be increased from 30 percent of cropped area in 2016-17 to 40 percent in 2017-18 and 50 percent in 2018-19. The Budget provision of ₹ 5,500 crore for this Yojana in 2016-17 (budget estimates) was increased to ₹ 13,240 crore in 2016-17 (revised estimates) to settle the arrear claims. For 2017-18, I have provided a sum of ₹ 9,000 crore. The sum insured under this Yojana has more than doubled from ₹ 69,000 crore in kharif 2015 to ₹ 1,41,625 crore in kharif 2016". [2]

Commenting on the *Fasal Bima Yojana,* NITI Aayog has stated, "Natural disasters such as droughts, floods, cyclones, storms, landslides and earthquakes can lead to extreme distress and hardship among many small farmers who lead a subsistence existence. In these situations, they need at least a minimal amount of relief at a rapid pace. The Pradhan Mantri Fasal Bima Yojana, for which ₹ 9,000 crore have been allotted in the 2017-18 Union Budget is an important positive step towards risk mitigation for farmers but it needs to be subjected to four important reforms. First, at present, the insurance scheme limits the farmers' contribution towards premium to 1.5 percent-2 percent of the sum insured for non-commercial crops and 5 percent of the sum insured for commercial crops irrespective of the sum insured. The government pays the remainder of the premium as subsidy. This model results in larger absolute subsidy amounts for larger farmers who are less vulnerable. The scheme should instead be modified to have a capped subsidy amount per farm household and any farmer desiring to insure larger sums should pay full premium for the difference. Second, insurance scheme should provide coverage for three to five years so that coverage extends to both good and bad years. Otherwise, insurance companies will have an incentive to go slow in selling policies during years that droughts are predicted. Third, the subsidy on the premium should take the form of direct benefit transfer to ensure that farmers can shop for the best value for their money. Finally, there should be minimally two companies offering insurance in any given location. This will create competition and lead to greater efficiency and lower premiums for farmers". [3]

8.5 Pradhan Mantri Kisan Samman Nidhi (PM-KISAN)

To provide an assured income support to the small and marginal farmers, the Finance Minister, while presenting Interim Budget for 2019-20 in the Parliament, announced a historic programme, namely PM-KISAN. Under this programme, vulnerable landholding farmer families, having cultivable land up to 2 hectares, will be provided direct income support at the rate of ₹ 6,000 per year. This income support will be transferred directly into the bank accounts of beneficiary farmers, in three equal instalments of ₹ 2,000 each. This programme will be funded by Government of India. Around 12 crore small and marginal farmer families are expected to benefit from this. The programme was made effective from December 1, 2018 and the first instalment for the period up to March 31, 2019 was paid during 2018-19 itself. This programme will entail an annual expenditure of ₹ 75,000 crore.

PM-KISAN not only provides assured supplemental income to the most vulnerable farmer families, but also meets their emergent needs especially before the harvest season. PM-KISAN paves the way for the farmers to earn and live a respectable living.

After assuming office for the second time on May 30, 2019, Prime Minister Narendra Modi chaired the first meeting of the Union Cabinet on May 31, 2019 and decided to extend PM-KISAN to allow all eligible farmers to avail benefit under this scheme. Thus, an estimated 2 crore more farmers were added to the scheme, taking the total number of beneficiaries to 14.5 crore.

In the wake of Covid-19, in March 2020, Government transferred ₹ 17,986 crore to farmers under the PM-Kisan scheme. Instalments due for the period of April 1 to July 31, 2020 were paid to 8.13 crore beneficiaries.

8.6 Pradhan Mantri Kisan Maandhan Yojana (PMKMY)

PM-KMY was launched on September 12, 2019 to expand the social security net to small and marginal farmers. It ensures minimum fixed pension of ₹ 3,000 to eligible landholding small and marginal farmers, on attaining the age of 60 years.

Endnotes

1. Government of India, Ministry of Finance, Budget Papers (2018-19), *Speech of the Finance Minister*, paras 13 to 15.
2. Government of India, Ministry of Finance, *Budget Speech of the Finance Minister 2017-18*, para 24.
3. NITI Aayog, *India: Three Year Action Agenda (2017-18 to 2019-20)*, August 2017, p. 32.

9

Cooking Fuel for the Poor

Till recently, the poor in India had limited access to liquefied petroleum gas (LPG), commonly called cooking gas. The spread of LPG cylinders was predominantly in the urban and semi-urban areas with the coverage mostly in middle class and affluent households. The poor had to rely on firewood, coal, dung cakes etc. as primary source of cooking. The smoke from burning such fuels caused alarming household pollution and adversely affected the health of women and children, causing several respiratory diseases/disorders. In addition, women and children had to go through the drudgery of collecting firewood.

Unclean cooking fuels led to premature deaths due to non-communicable diseases such as heart disease, stroke, chronic obstructive pulmonary disease and lung cancer. Indoor air pollution is also responsible for a significant number of acute respiratory illnesses in young children. According to World Health Organization (WHO), smoke inhaled by women from unclean fuel is equivalent to burning 400 cigarettes in an hour.

9.1 Pradhan Mantri Ujjwala Yojana (PMUY)

PMUY was launched by Prime Minister Narendra Modi on May 1, 2016 in Ballia, Uttar Pradesh. Under this scheme, LPG connections are provided to below poverty line (BPL) families with a support of ₹ 1,600 per connection. Ensuring women's empowerment, especially in rural India, the connections is issued in the name of women of the households. Identification of the BPL families will be done through socio-economic caste census data.

9.1.1 Objectives of the Scheme: PMUY aims to safeguard the health of women and children by providing them with a clean cooking fuel (LPG), so that they do not have to compromise their health in smoky kitchens or wander in unsafe areas collecting firewood.

PMUY is likely to result in an additional employment of around 1 lakh and provide business opportunity of at least ₹ 10,000 crore over the next 3 years to the Indian industry. Launch of this scheme has provided a great boost to the Make in India campaign as all the manufacturers of cylinders, gas stoves, regulators, and gas hoses are domestic.

The launch of PMUY in Ballia was followed by launch of the scheme in Dahod in Gujarat. PMUY has also been launched in several districts in UP and Bihar.

Providing LPG connections to BPL households will ensure universal coverage of cooking gas in the country. This measure will empower women and protect their health. It will reduce drudgery and the time spent on cooking. It will also provide employment for rural youth in the supply chain of cooking gas.

9.1.2 Main Features of the Scheme: These are as under:

1. Under the scheme, 5 crore LPG connections are to be provided to BPL households. The identification of eligible BPL families will be made in consultation with the State Governments and the Union Territories.
2. BPL is a person/household who suffers from at least one deprivation under the Socio-Economic Caste Census (SECC), 2011 (Rural) Database. For identifying urban poor, separate instructions are to be issued.
3. While the selection of beneficiaries would be from the BPL families only, preference would be given to SC/ST and weaker sections of society.
4. While providing the new connections to BPL households, priority would be given to the States which have lower LPG coverage (compared to the national average) as on January 1, 2016.
5. Release of LPG connection under this scheme shall be in the name of the women belonging to the BPL family.
6. The scheme would be implemented over 3 years, namely

2016-17, 2017-18 and 2018-19 across the country.

7. The scheme provides a financial support of ₹ 1,600 for each LPG connection to the BPL households. The administrative cost of ₹ 1,600 per connection, which includes a cylinder, pressure regulator, booklet, safety hose etc., would be borne by the Government.
8. A woman of the BPL household, which does not have access to LPG connection may apply for a new LPG connection (in the prescribed format) to the LPG distributor.
9. Benefits of the scheme have been extended to people of all Hilly States including North-East States by treating them as *priority states*. This step will effectively address the difficulties being faced by poor people—residing in the States of Jammu and Kashmir, Himachal Pradesh, Uttarakhand, Sikkim, Assam, Nagaland, Manipur, Mizoram, Arunachal Pradesh, Meghalaya and Tripura—in accessing LPG for cooking purposes.

9.1.3 Ujjwala Yojna in the Budget for 2018-19: Finance Minister Arun Jaitley in his budget speech to the Parliament on February 1, 2018 announced, "We launched Prime Minister's Ujjwala Scheme to make poor women free from the smoke of wood. Initially our target was to provide free LPG connections to about 5 crore poor women. But in view of the pace of implementation of Ujjwala scheme and its popularity among the women, we propose to increase the target of providing free connection to 8 crore poor women". [1]

9.2 PAHAL: Direct Benefit Transfer for LPG Consumer (DBTL) Scheme

Government, as a measure of good governance, has introduced well-targeted system of subsidy delivery to LPG consumers through PAHAL. This initiative of the Government is aimed at rationalizing subsidies to cut subsidy leakages, but not subsidies themselves. PAHAL has entered into Guinness Book of World Records, being the largest Direct Benefit

Transfer Scheme.

Every household in the country is entitled to 12 LPG cylinders of 14.2 kg. each at subsidised rates in a year. The amount of subsidy is transferred directly in bank accounts of beneficiaries as a part of extension of Direct Benefit Transfer (DBT) scheme. Any requirement beyond that is to be purchased at market price (non-subsidised LPG rates).

PAHAL has helped in identifying ghost/multiple/inactive accounts. Blocking of such accounts has resulted in considerable savings on the part of Government. Further, Government has taken steps to rationalise the subsidy outgo by excluding such LPG consumers or his/her spouse having taxable income of above ₹ 10 lakh, from availing LPG subsidy.

Oil firms revise LPG price on first of every month based on average benchmark rate and foreign exchange rate in the previous month.

Besides supplying domestic LPG cylinders to households, oil companies also market commercial LPG cylinders in 19 kg. and 47.5 kg. capacity. The commercial LPG cylinders are available at market rates and customers can avail of the superior energy efficiency of LPG in their commercial establishments like canteens, hotels or even in industrial and fabrication works like cutting, welding, heating etc.

LPG cylinders used in households are red coloured. LPG cylinders used in commercial and industrial establishments are purple in colour.

Goods and services tax (GST) on LPG is calculated at market rate of the fuel. The Government may choose to subsidise a part of the price but tax will have to be paid at market rates. This means that GST is calculated every month on the rate at which domestic non-subsidised LPG is priced.

9.3 Pradhan Mantri Garib Kalyan Yojana (PMGKY)

In the wake of COVID-19 pandemic, a ₹ 1.7 lakh crore welfare package was announced on March 26, 2020 under the

Pradhan Mantri Garib Kalyan Yojana (PMGKY) to provide 3 LPG cylinders free (April, May and June of 2020) to over 8 crore beneficiaries of the Pradhan Mantri Ujjawala Yojana (PMUY).

9.4 Direct Transfer of Cash Subsidy on Public Distribution System (PDS) Kerosene

The Centre allocates subsidised kerosene to the States and Union Territories as affordable cooking fuel for domestic use, mainly to those living below the poverty line.

The Ministry of Oil and Natural Gas has introduced Direct Benefit Transfer through which subsidy is transferred directly to the bank accounts of the beneficiaries, who purchase PDS kerosene at non-subsidised rate. The Aadhaar card has been made mandatory for government subsidy on purchase of kerosene.

Implementation of the scheme is expected to result in better subsidy management through direct transfer of subsidy into bank accounts of beneficiaries. This would result in reducing expenditure on subsidy and also help in curbing diversion of subsidized kerosene.

However, States and Union Territories are encouraged to become *kerosene free* by bringing all households under LPG.

Endnote

1. Government of India, Ministry of Finance, Budget Papers (2018-19), *Speech of the Finance Minister*, para 38.

10

Pradhan Mantri Aawas Yojana (PMAY): Housing for All (HFA)

Housing is an activity that is typically labour intensive and, therefore, fits in well with the pattern of development envisaged for India. The provision of shelter is a basic need which must be met. Housing construction also creates much-needed employment for the unskilled and, therefore, income for the relatively poor.

According to 'Drinking Water, Sanitation, Hygiene and Housing Condition' survey of NSS (76th round) conducted during July-December 2018, about 96.0 percent of the households in the rural areas and about 63.8 percent of the households in the urban areas had own dwelling unit.

Among the households living in houses, about 96.7 percent of the households in the rural areas and about 91.5 percent of the households in the urban areas used the house for residential purpose only.

Among the households living in houses, about 89.0 percent of the households in the rural areas and about 56.4 percent of the households in the urban areas had independent house.

Among the households living in houses, about 76.7 percent of the households in the rural areas and about 96.0 percent of the households in the urban areas had the house of pucca structure.

10.1 PMAY—Urban

HFA (Urban Mission) was launched in June 2015 to provide housing to all in urban areas by 2022. Under this Mission, it is planned to build 2 crore houses for urban poor including economically weaker sections (EWS) and low income groups (LIGs). Along with the targets of 6,15,649 households in 2015-16 and 15,24,360 households in 2016-17, a total 94,97,398 households are targeted to be covered by 2019-20.

10.1.1 Objective and Scope of Housing for All (HFA): HFA is a programme launched by the Ministry of Housing and Urban Poverty Alleviation (MoHUPA), in Mission mode which envisions provision of Housing for All by 2022 when India completes 75 years of its Independence. The Mission seeks to address the housing requirement of urban poor including slum dwellers through following programme verticals:

1. Slum rehabilitation of slum dwellers with participation of private developers using land as a resource.
2. Promotion of affordable housing for weaker sections through credit-linked subsidy.
3. Affordable housing in partnership with public and private sectors.
4. Subsidy for beneficiary-led individual house construction.

10.1.2 Coverage and Duration of HFA: All 4041 statutory towns as per Census 2011 with focus on 500 class I cities would be covered in three phases as follows:

1. Phase I (April 2015 to March 2017) to cover 100 cities selected from States/UTs as per their willingness.
2. Phase II (April 2017 to March 2019) to cover additional 200 cities.
3. Phase III (April 2019 to March 2022) to cover all other remaining cities.

Ministry, however, will have flexibility regarding inclusion of additional cities in earlier phases in case there is a resource backed demand from States/UTs.

10.1.3 Financial Support: HFA Mission will provide financial support to the States for the preparation of Housing for All Plan of Action (HFAPoA). The Mission will assist States/cities in carrying out the activities for preparation of HFAPoA under capacity building and A&OE funds. States and cities which have already been given assistance under erstwhile Rajiv Awas Yojana (RAY) for preparation of Slum Free City Plan of Action (SFCPoA) should utilise that amount for preparation of HFAPoA and claim next instalment when 70 percent of the released funds have been utilised.

HFAPoA addresses urban poor who may not necessarily be slum dwellers and it is thus required to integrate all four programme verticals of the HFA Mission whereas SFCPoA was linked only to slum dwellers.

The activities required for preparation of HFAPoA will be funded by MoHUPA in the ratio of 75:25 and in case of North Eastern and special category States in the ratio of 90:10. The unit cost/financial norms for different activities will be determined by CSMC and till then the existing norms under RAY should be used.

10.1.4 Administrative Requirements: MoHUPA will provide assistance to the states and city governments for enhancing capacity of their employees/officers in the operational areas like planning, engineering, social mobilisation, financial planning etc.

MoHUPA will also assist city and State Governments in the constitution of technical and project management cell at state and city level.

1. A State Level Technical Cell (SLTC) with 5-10 professionals.
2. A City Level Technical Cell (CLTC) with 2-4 professionals depending on the size of the city and quantum of work. In case of big cities like metropolitan cities the number of professionals in CLTC can be more than 4 with the approval of CSMC.
3. The following expertise is to be mandatorily provided in the respective SLTCs and CLTCs:

- Urban Planning/Town Planning Specialist.
- Housing Finance Specialist.
- Building Technology Specialist.

4. CSMC can increase the size of such cell on the requirement of State/UT.

5. MoHUPA support for CLTC and SLTC will be in the ratio of 75:25 and in case of North-Eastern and special categories states it will be in the ratio of 90:10.
6. The financial norms for such Cells will be prescribed by CSMC and till the time CSMC prescribes these norms, the norms already approved under RAY will be applicable.

Any other activities which is required for building the capacity for implementing the Mission or in general for augmenting the capacity of Centre, States and ULBs in this sector can be taken up with the approval of CSMC.

10.1.5 Beneficiary under Housing for All: A beneficiary is defined as a family comprising of husband, wife and unmarried children. Such beneficiary should not own a pucca house either in his/her name or in the name of any member of his/her family in any part of India to receive central assistance under the Mission. EWS category of beneficiaries is eligible for assistance in all four verticals of the Missions whereas LIG category is eligible under only CLSS component of the Mission.

The EWS/LIG categories are defined as follows:

1. EWS households with an annual income up to ₹ 3 lakh.
2. LIG households with an annual income between ₹ 3 lakh to ₹ 6 lakh.

States/UTs have flexibility to redefine the annual income criteria as per local needs with the approval of Ministry.

For identification as an EWS or LIG beneficiary under the scheme, an individual loan applicant will submit self-certificate/affidavit as proof of income.

Under the mission, a beneficiary can avail of benefit of one component only.

A slum is defined as a compact area of at least 300 people or about 60-70 households of poorly built congested tenements in unhygienic environment usually with inadequate infrastructure and lacking in proper sanitary and drinking water facilities. This is also the definition of Slums as per Census 2011.

A house is defined as an all-weather single unit or a unit in a multi-storeyed super structure having carpet area of up to 30 square metres for EWS category and up to 60 square metres for LIG category with adequate basic civic services and infrastructure services like toilet, water, electricity etc.

States/UTs will have flexibility in terms of determining the size of house and other facilities at the state level in consultation with the Ministry but without any enhanced financial assistance from Centre.

10.1.6 Primary Lending Institutions: Primary lending institutions are scheduled commercial banks, housing finance companies, regional rural banks (RRBs), state co-operative banks, urban co-operative banks or any other institutions as may be identified by the MoHUPA.

A. Affordable Housing through Credit-linked Subsidy: Under credit-linked subsidy, beneficiaries of economically weaker section (EWS) and low income group (LIG) can seek housing loans from banks, housing finance companies and other such institutions for new construction and enhancement to existing dwellings as incremental housing. The credit-linked subsidy will be available only for loan amounts up to ₹ 6 lakh and such loans would be eligible for an interest subsidy at the rate of 6.5 percent for tenure of 15 years or during tenure of loan whichever is lower. The net present value (NPV) of the interest subsidy will be calculated at a discount rate of 9 percent. Any additional loans beyond ₹ 6 lakh, will be at non-subsidized rate. Interest subsidy will be credited upfront to the loan account of beneficiaries through lending institutions resulting in reduced effective housing loan and equated monthly instalment (EMI).

The subsidy would be released by the central nodal agencies (CNAs) based on the disbursements made by PLIs to the beneficiaries. Subsidy, so disbursed by the CNA to the PLI, will be credited by the PLI to the borrower's account upfront by deducting it from the principal loan amount. As a result, the borrower will pay EMI on the remainder of the principal loan amount. For example, the borrower avails a loan for ₹ 6 lakh and subsidy thereon works out to ₹ 2 lakh, the amount (₹ 2 lakh) would be reduced upfront from the loan (i.e. the loan would reduce to ₹ 4 lakh) and the borrower would pay EMIs on the reduced amount of ₹ 4 lakh.

10.1.7 Preferential Treatment: Preference under the Scheme will be given to manual scavengers, women (with overriding preference to widows), persons belonging to scheduled castes/scheduled tribes/other backward classes, minorities, persons with disabilities and transgenders subject to beneficiaries being from EWS/LIG segments.

10.1.8 Monitoring and Evaluation (M&E): Mission will be monitored at all three levels: City, State and Central Government. CSMC will monitor formulation of HFAPoA, annual implementation plans (AIPs) and project implementation. Suitable monitoring mechanisms will be developed by the Mission. States and cities will also be required to develop monitoring mechanism for monitoring the progress of mission and its different components.

10.2 PMAY—Gramin

To address the gaps in rural housing and in view of Government's commitment to provide Housing for All by 2022, Indira Awaas Yojana (IAY) was re-structured into Pradhan Mantri Awaas Yojana–Gramin (PMAY-G) w.e.f. April 1, 2016.

10.2.1 Objective of PMAY-G: PMAY-G aims to provide a pucca house with basic amenities to all houseless and households living in kutcha and dilapidated house by 2022. The immediate objective is to cover 1 crore households living in kutcha house/dilapidated houses in three years from 2016-17 to 2018-19 and ensure construction of quality houses.

10.2.2 Salient Features of PMAY-G: These are as under:

1. Providing assistance for construction of 1 crore houses in rural areas over the period of 3 years from 2016-17 to 2018-19.

2. Minimum unit (house) size enhanced from the existing 20 square metres to 25 square metres including a dedicated area for hygienic cooking.
3. Enhancement of unit assistance from ₹ 70,000 to ₹ 1.20 lakh in plains and from ₹ 75,000 to ₹ 1.30 lakh in hilly states, and difficult areas.
4. The cost of unit (house) assistance is to be shared between Central and State Governments in the ratio 60:40 in plain areas and 90:10 for north-eastern and hilly states.
5. Identification of beneficiaries using Socio-Economic and Caste Census, 2011 data (SECC-2011 data). The identification and selection of the beneficiaries shall be done by the community through the Gram Sabha, from the SECC 2011 list, based on the housing deficiency and other social deprivation parameters.
6. Setting up of National Technical Support Agency at national level to provide technical support in achieving the target set under the project. The beneficiaries of PMAY-G in addition to being provided financial assistance shall also be offered technical assistance in the construction of the house.
7. If the beneficiary so chooses, he/she will be facilitated to avail loan from financial institutions for an amount of up to ₹ 70,000.
8. Meeting the additional financial requirement by borrowing through National Bank for Agriculture and Rural Development (NABARD) to be amortised through budgetary grant after 2022.
9. Special projects to be sanctioned to states based on situational exigencies and special needs.

10.2.3 Exclusion and Inclusion:

A. Exclusion of Pucca Houses: All households living in houses with pucca roof and/or pucca wall and households living in houses with more than 2 rooms are filtered out.

B. Automatic Exclusion: From the remaining set of households, all households fulfilling any one of the 13 parameters listed below are automatically excluded:

1. Motorised two/three/four wheeler/fishing boat.
2. Mechanised three/four wheeler agricultural equipment.
3. Kisan Credit Card with credit limit of ₹ 50,000 or above.
4. Household with any member as a Government employee.
5. Households with non-agricultural enterprises registered with the Government.
6. Any member of the family earning more than ₹ 10,000 per month.
7. Paying income tax.
8. Paying professional tax.
9. Own a refrigerator.
10. Own landline phone.
11. Own 2.5 acres or more of irrigated land with at least one irrigation equipment.
12. 5 acres or more of irrigated land for two or more crop seasons.
13. Owning at least 7.5 acres of land or more with at least one irrigation equipment.

C. Criteria for Automatic Inclusion: These are as under:

1. Households without shelter.
2. Destitute/living on alms.
3. Manual scavengers.
4. Primitive Tribal Groups.
5. Legally released bonded labourer.

11

National Health Policy (NHP), 2017 and Ayushman Bharat

11.1 National Health Policy (NHP), 2017

NHP, 2017 was launched by the Ministry of Health and Family Welfare on March 15, 2017.Through the help of this policy, Government aims to shift focus from *sick-care* to *wellness*. It aims at providing healthcare in an *assured manner* to all by addressing current and emerging challenges arising from the ever changing socio-economic, epidemiological and technological scenarios. NHP, 2017 seeks to reach everyone in a comprehensive integrated way to move towards wellness. It aims at achieving universal health coverage and delivering quality healthcare services to all at affordable cost.

The primary aim of the NHP, 2017, is to inform, clarify, strengthen and prioritize the role of the Government in shaping health systems in all its dimensions—investments in health, organization of healthcare services, prevention of diseases and promotion of good health through cross-sectoral actions, access to technologies, developing human resources, encouraging medical pluralism, building knowledge base, developing better financial protection strategies, strengthening regulation and health assurance.

11.1.1 Goal: The policy envisages the attainment of highest possible level of health and well-being for all at all ages, through a preventive and promotive healthcare orientation in all developmental policies, and universal access to good quality healthcare services without anyone having to face financial hardship as a consequence. This would be achieved through increasing access, improving quality and lowering the cost of healthcare delivery.

11.1.2 Key Policy Principles: These are as under:

1. **Professionalism, Integrity and Ethics:** The health policy commits itself to the highest professional standards, integrity and ethics to be maintained in the entire system of health care delivery in the country, supported by a credible, transparent and responsible regulatory environment.
2. **Equity:** Reducing inequity would mean affirmative action to reach the poorest. It would mean minimizing disparity on account of gender, poverty, caste, disability, other forms of social exclusion and geographical barriers. It would imply greater investments and financial protection for the poor who suffer the largest burden of disease.
3. **Affordability:** As costs of care increases, affordability, as distinct from equity, requires emphasis. Catastrophic household health care expenditures defined as health expenditure exceeding 10 percent of its total monthly consumption expenditure or 40 percent of its monthly non-food consumption expenditure, are unacceptable.
4. **Universality:** Prevention of exclusions on social, economic or on grounds of current health status. In this backdrop, systems and services are envisaged to be designed to cater to the entire population including special groups.
5. **Patient Centred and Quality of Care:** Gender sensitive, effective, safe, and convenient healthcare services to be provided with dignity and confidentiality. There is need to evolve and disseminate standards and guidelines for all levels of facilities and a system to ensure that the quality of healthcare is not compromised.
6. **Accountability:** Financial and performance accountability, transparency in decision making, and elimination of corruption in health care systems, both in public and private.
7. **Inclusive Partnerships:** A multi-stakeholder approach with partnership and participation of all non-health ministries and communities. This approach would include partnerships with academic institutions, not-for-profit agencies, and health care industry as well.

8. **Pluralism:** Patients who so choose and when appropriate, would have access to AYUSH care providers based on documented and validated local, home and community based practices. These systems, *inter alia*, would also have Government support in research and supervision to develop and enrich their contribution to meeting the national health goals and objectives through integrative practices.
9. **Decentralization:** Decentralisation of decision making to a level as is consistent with practical considerations and institutional capacity. Community participation in health planning processes, to be promoted side by side.
10. **Dynamism and Adaptiveness:** Constantly improving dynamic organization of health care based on new knowledge and evidence with learning from the communities and from national and international knowledge partners is designed.

11.1.3 Objectives: Improve health status through concerted policy action in all sectors and expand preventive, promotive, curative, palliative and rehabilitative services provided through the public health sector with focus on quality.

A. Progressively Achieve Universal Health Coverage:

1. Assuring availability of free, comprehensive primary health care services, for all aspects of reproductive, maternal, child and adolescent health and for the most prevalent communicable, non-communicable and occupational diseases in the population. The Policy also envisages optimum use of existing manpower and infrastructure as available in the health sector and advocates collaboration with non -government sector on pro-bono basis for delivery of health care services linked to a health card to enable every family to have access to a doctor of their choice from amongst those volunteering their services.
2. Ensuring improved access and affordability, of quality secondary and tertiary care services through a combination of public hospitals and well measured strategic purchasing

of services in health care deficit areas, from private care providers, especially the not-for profit providers

3. Achieving a significant reduction in out of pocket expenditure due to health care costs and achieving reduction in proportion of households experiencing catastrophic health expenditures and consequent impoverishment.

B. Reinforcing Trust in Public Healthcare System: Strengthening the trust of the common man in public health care system by making it predictable, efficient, patient centric, affordable and effective, with a comprehensive package of services and products that meet immediate health care needs of most people.

C. Align the Growth of Private Healthcare Sector with Public Health Goals: Influence the operation and growth of the private health care sector and medical technologies to ensure alignment with public health goals. Enable private sector contribution to making health care systems more effective, efficient, rational, safe, affordable and ethical. Strategic purchasing by the Government to fill critical gaps in public health facilities would create a demand for private health care sector, in alignment with the public health goals.

11.1.4 Specific Quantitative Goals and Objectives: The indicative, quantitative goals and objectives are outlined under three broad components:

1. Health status and programme impact.
2. Health systems performance.
3. Health system strengthening.

These goals and objectives are aligned to achieve sustainable development in health sector in keeping with the policy thrust.

A. Health Status and Programme Impact:

(a) Life Expectancy and Healthy Life:

1. Increase life expectancy at birth from 67.5 to 70 by 2025.
2. Establish regular tracking of Disability Adjusted Life Years (DALY) Index as a measure of burden of disease and its trends by major categories by 2022.

3. Reduction of TFR to 2.1 at national and sub-national level by 2025.

(b) Mortality by Age and/or Cause:

1. Reduce under five mortality to 23 by 2025 and MMR from current levels to 100 by 2020.
2. Reduce infant mortality rate to 28 by 2019.
3. Reduce neo-natal mortality to 16 and still birth rate to "single digit" by 2025.

(c) Reduction of Disease Prevalence/Incidence:

1. Achieve global target of 2020 which is also termed as target of 90:90:90, for HIV/AIDS, i.e. 90 percent of all people living with HIV know their HIV status, 90 percent of all people diagnosed with HIV infection receive sustained antiretroviral therapy and 90 percent of all people receiving antiretroviral therapy will have viral suppression.
2. Achieve and maintain elimination status of Leprosy by 2018, Kala-Azar by 2017 and Lymphatic Filariasis in endemic pockets by 2017.
3. To achieve and maintain a cure rate of >85 percent in new sputum positive patients for TB and reduce incidence of new cases, to reach elimination status by 2025.
4. To reduce the prevalence of blindness to 0.25/1000 by 2025 and disease burden by one third from current levels.
5. To reduce premature mortality from cardiovascular diseases, cancer, diabetes or chronic respiratory diseases by 25 percent by 2025.

B. Health Systems Performance:

(a) Coverage of Health Services:

1. Increase utilization of public health facilities by 50 percent from current levels by 2025.
2. Antenatal care coverage to be sustained above 90 percent and skilled attendance at birth above 90 percent by 2025.
3. More than 90 percent of the newborn are fully immunized by one year of age by 2025.
4. Meet need of family planning above 90 percent at national

and sub- national level by 2025.

5. 80 percent of known hypertensive and diabetic individuals at household level maintain "controlled disease status" by 2025.

(b) Cross-sectoral Goals Related to Health:

1. Relative reduction in prevalence of current tobacco use by 15 percent by 2020 and 30 percent by 2025.
2. Reduction of 40 percent in prevalence of stunting of under-five children by 2025.
3. Access to safe water and sanitation to all by 2020 (Swachh Bharat Mission).
4. Reduction of occupational injury by half from current levels of 334 per lakh agricultural workers by 2020.
5. National/ State level tracking of selected health behaviour.

C. Health Systems Strengthening:

(a) Health Finance:

1. Increase health expenditure by Government as a percent of GDP from the existing 1.15 percent to 2.5 percent by 2025.
2. Increase State sector health spending to >8 percent of their budget by 2020.
3. Decrease in proportion of households facing catastrophic health expenditure from the current levels by 25 percent by 2025.

(b) Health Infrastructure and Human Resource:

1. Ensure availability of paramedics and doctors as per Indian Public Health Standard (IPHS) norm in high priority districts by 2020.
2. Increase community health volunteers to population ratio as per IPHS norm, in high priority districts by 2025.
3. Establish primary and secondary care facility as per norms in high priority districts (population as well as time to reach norms) by 2025.

(c) Health Management Information:

1. Ensure district-level electronic database of information on health system components by 2020.

2. Strengthen the health surveillance system and establish registries for diseases of public health importance by 2020.
3. Establish federated integrated health information architecture, Health Information Exchanges and National Health Information Network by 2025.

In short, National Health Policy (NHP), 2017, envisages comprehensive primary health care delivered through HWCs. The policy also commits that two-thirds or more of government spending will be targeted at primary care. Additionally, the announcement of Ayushman Bharat by the government is a game changer.

11.2 Ayushman Bharat

Ayushman Bharat is a flagship programme of the Government of India which comprises of the following two interrelated components:

1. Establishment of Health and Wellness Centres (HWCs) for delivering comprehensive primary healthcare.
2. Pradhan Mantri Jan Arogya Yojana (PMJAY), a health assurance scheme for preventing the financial hardships in availing in-patient care.

This is the strategy adopted by India to achieve the vision of Universal Health Coverage (UHC) with its underlying commitment of *leaving no one behind*.

11.2.1 Health and Wellness Centres (HWCs): The National Health Policy, 2017 recommends strengthening the delivery of primary healthcare, through establishment of HWCs and calls for a commitment of two-third of the health budget for comprehensive primary healthcare. Government of India announced upgradation of 1,50,000 sub-centres and primary health centres to HWCs by 2022 under Ayushman Bharat. This initiative is an attempt to move from selective and segmented approach to a comprehensive need-based health care service delivery.

HWCs provide preventive, promotive, rehabilitative and curative care for reproductive, maternal, new born, child plus adolescent health (RMNCH+A), communicable diseases, non-communicable diseases, ophthalmology, ENT, trauma services etc. HWCs would undertake population based screening, prevention and control for common non-communicable diseases—hypertension, diabetes, and the three common cancers (oral, cervix and breast cancer), building on the already existing National Programme for the Prevention and Control of Cancer, Diabetes, Cardiovascular Diseases and Stroke (NPCDCS). HWC would be the first point of contact with the PHC/CHC serving as the first referral point. This would, over time, reduce the burden on secondary and tertiary centres having to provide care for primary health as well, and also reduce out of pocket expenditures.

11.2.2 Pradhan Mantri Jan Arogya Yojana (PMJAY): PMJAY, the largest public health insurance scheme in the world, aims at providing financial protection (Swasthya Suraksha) to 10.74 crore poor and vulnerable families (approximately 50 crore beneficiaries). The scheme offers a benefit cover of ₹ 5 lakh per family per year (on a family floater basis). PMJAY covers medical and hospitalization expenses for most of the secondary and tertiary care procedures. PMJAY has defined 1,350 medical packages covering surgery, medical and certain day care treatments including medicines, diagnostics and transport.

To ensure that nobody is left out (especially the girl child, women, children and elderly), there is no cap on family size and age in the scheme. The scheme is cashless and paperless at public hospitals and empanelled private hospitals. The benefits also include pre- and post-hospitalization expenses. The scheme is entitlement based.

11.3 New Initiatives for Maternal and New born Health

11.3.1 Laqshya: This quality improvement initiative was launched in December 2017 with the objectives of reducing preventable maternal and new born mortality, morbidity and stillbirths associated with the care around delivery in labour room and maternity operation theatre and to ensure respectful maternity care. Laqshya initiative is a focused and targeted approach to strengthen key processes related to the labour rooms and maternity operation theatres in order to achieve time-bound targets and to ensure desired outcome within a short period.

11.3.2 Midwifery Initiative: The Government initiated midwifery services throughout the country in 2018, with an objective to provide access to quality maternal and new born health services, promote natural birthing, ensure respectful care and reduce over medication. The midwifery services initiative aims to create a cadre for nurse practitioners in midwifery who are skilled, knowledgeable and capable of providing compassionate women-centric pregnancy care.

11.3.3 Pradhan Mantri Surakshit Matritva Abhiyan (PMSMA): PMSMA) was launched in 2016 to provide comprehensive and quality ante-natal care (ANC) to pregnant women on the 9th of every month. Under PMSMA, doctors from both the public and private sector examine pregnant women on 9th of every month at Government health facilities. So far, more than 1.8 crore ante-natal check-ups (in addition to routine four ANC check-ups) have been conducted across the country under this programme.

12

Micro Units Development and Refinance Agency (MUDRA) and Pradhan Mantri MUDRA Yojana (PMMY)

Small enterprises are at the heart of employment generation and decentralization of economic power in India. However, facilitation from the Government is required to minimise the transaction costs of technology upgradation, market penetration, and modernisation of infrastructure. The sector is suffering from quite a few impediments, which need to be addressed immediately to make small businesses a hub of entrepreneurship and innovations.

12.1 What is MUDRA?

MUDRA is a non-banking financial company (NBFC) which supports development of micro enterprise sector in India. It provides refinance support to banks/micro finance institutions (MFIs) for lending to micro units having loan requirement up to ₹ 10 lakh. MUDRA provides refinance to micro business under Pradhan Mantri MUDRA Yojana. The other products of MUDRA are meant for development support to the micro enterprise sector.

12.2 Services Offered by MUDRA

The services offered by MUDRA—targeted across the spectrum of beneficiary segments—can be categorized as below:

1. Technology enabler.
2. Refinance for micro units to commercial banks, non-banking financial companies (NBFCs), regional rural banks (RRBs), co-operative banks and micro finance institutions (MFIs).

- Shishu: up to ₹ 50,000
- Kishor: above ₹ 50,000 and up to ₹ 5 lakh.
- Tarun: above ₹ 5 lakh and up to ₹ 10 lakh.

3. Credit guarantee to MUDRA loans.
4. Development and promotional support.

- Sectoral development.
- Skill development.
- Entrepreneurship development.
- Financial literacy.
- Institution development.

12.3 Pradhan Mantri MUDRA Yojana (PMMY)

Under the aegis of PMMY, MUDRA has created products/schemes. The interventions have been named *Shishu*, *Kishor* and *Tarun* to signify the stage of growth/development and funding needs of the beneficiary micro unit/entrepreneur and also to provide a reference point for the next phase of graduation/growth to look forward to:

1. Shishu: covering loans up to ₹ 50,000.
2. Kishor: covering loans above ₹ 50,000 and up to ₹ 5 lakh.
3. Tarun: covering loans above ₹ 5 lakh and up to ₹ 10 lakh.

It is ensured that more focus is given to Shishu category units and then to Kishor and Tarun categories.

Within the framework and overall objective of development and growth of micro enterprises sector under Shishu, Kishor and Tarun, the products being offered by MUDRA are so designed as to meet the requirements of different sectors/business activities as well as business/entrepreneur segments.

Traditional financing in Indian context adopts an asset-based lending approach with emphasis on collaterals. Micro units, most of the times, are unable to provide the comfort of collaterals. Hence MUDRA loans, i.e. loans up to ₹ 10 lakh, have been made collateral free, as per the Reserve Bank of India (RBI) norms in this regard.

To mitigate the issue of collaterals, MUDRA offers a credit guarantee product. MUDRA credit guarantee is extended by creation of a fund called Credit Guarantee Fund for Micro Units (CGFMU) and the scheme was notified by Government of India on April 18, 2016. Accordingly, all eligible micro loans sanctioned since April 8, 2015 are covered under the scheme. The scheme is being managed by National Credit Guarantee Trustee Company (NCGTC), an agency promoted by the Government of India.

Since the individual loan sizes are small and number of loans large, MUDRA credit guarantee scheme provides a portfolio guarantee. Under this, credit guarantee or risk sharing is provided for a portfolio of homogenous loans instead of a scheme for individual loan-by-loan guarantee. This is expected to create administrative efficiencies and increase receptiveness for the credit guarantee product. The guarantee product is one of the key interventions proposed with the objective of bringing down the cost of funds for the end beneficiary to improve its creditworthiness.

The corpus for the credit guarantee scheme is regularly augmented with a charge on the outstanding loans under refinance. The same is utilized for providing first loss guarantee/credit enhancement for securitized portfolio loans.

The funding support from MUDRA is of four types:

1. Micro Credit Scheme (MCS).
2. Refinance Scheme.
3. Women Enterprise Programme.
4. Securitization of Loan Portfolio.

12.3.1 Micro Credit Scheme (MCS): MCS is offered mainly through micro finance institutions (MFIs), which deliver credit up to ₹ 1 lakh, for various micro enterprise activities. Although, the mode of delivery may be through groups like self-help groups (SHGs) and joint liability groups (JLGs), the loans are given to the individuals for specific income generating micro enterprise activity. For availing financial support, the MFIs need to enrol with MUDRA by complying with some of the requirements as notified by MUDRA, from time-to-time.

12.3.2 Refinance Scheme: Different banks like commercial banks, regional rural banks (RRBs) and scheduled co-operative banks are eligible to avail the refinance support from MUDRA for financing micro enterprise activities. The refinance is available for term loans and working capital loans, up to an amount of ₹ 10 lakh per unit. The eligible banks, which have enrolled with MUDRA by complying with the requirements as notified, can avail refinance from MUDRA for the loans issued under Shishu, Kishor and Tarun categories.

12.3.3 Women Enterprise Programme: In order to encourage women entrepreneurs, the financing banks/MFIs may consider extending additional facilities, including interest reduction on their loans. At present, MUDRA extends a reduction of 25 bps (i.e. 0.25 percent) in its interest rates to MFIs/NBFCs which are providing loans to women entrepreneurs.

12.3.4 Securitization of Loan Portfolio: MUDRA also supports banks, NBFCs and MFIs for raising funds for financing micro enterprises by participating in securitization of their loan assets against micro enterprise portfolio, by providing second loss default guarantee, for credit enhancement.

12.4 Purpose of MUDRA Loan

MUDRA loan is extended for a variety of purposes which help income generation and employment creation. The loans are extended mainly for the following activities:

1. Business loan for vendors, traders, shopkeepers and other service sector activities.
2. Working capital loan through MUDRA cards.
3. Equipment finance for micro units.
4. Transport vehicle loans.

Following is an illustrative list of the activities that can be covered under MUDRA loans:

12.4.1 Transport Vehicles: Purchase of transport vehicles for goods and personal transport such as auto rickshaw, small goods transport vehicle, 3-wheelers, e-rickshaw, passenger cars, taxis etc.

12.4.2 Community, Social and Personal Service Activities: Saloons, beauty parlours, gymnasium, boutiques, tailoring shops, dry cleaning, cycle and motorcycle repair shops, DTP and photocopying facilities, medicine shops, courier agents etc.

12.4.3 Food Products Sector: It includes the following:

1. Activities such as papad, achaar, jam and jelly making.
2. Agricultural produce preservation at rural level.
3. Sweet shops, small service food stalls and day-to-day catering/canteen services.
4. Cold chain vehicles, cold storages, ice and ice cream making units.
5. Biscuits, bread and bun making units.

12.4.4 Textile Products Sector/Activity: Following are included under it:

1. Handloom, powerloom, khadi, chikan work, zari and zardozi work.
2. Traditional embroidery and hand work, traditional dyeing and printing, apparel design, knitting etc.
3. Cotton ginning, computerized embroidery and stitching.
4. Non-garment products such as bags, vehicle accessories, furnishing accessories etc.

12.4.5 Business Loans for Traders and Shopkeepers: These include financial support for onward lending to individuals for running their shops, trading and business activities, service enterprises and non-farm income generating activities with beneficiary loan size of up to ₹ 10 lakh per enterprise/borrower.

12.4.6 Equipment Finance Scheme for Micro Units: It pertains to setting up micro enterprises by purchasing necessary machinery/equipments with per beneficiary loan size of up to ₹ 10 lakh.

12.4.7 Activities Allied to Agriculture: These include pisciculture, bee keeping, poultry, livestock, rearing, grading, sorting, aggregation agro industries, dairy, fisheries, agri-clinics and agribusiness centres, food and agro-processing etc.

(excluding crop loans, and loans for land improvement such as canal, irrigation and wells).

12.5 MUDRA Card

MUDRA card is an innovative product which provides working capital facility as a cash credit arrangement. MUDRA card is a debit card issued against the MUDRA loan account, for working capital portion of the loan. The borrower can make use of MUDRA card in multiple withdrawal and credit, so as to manage the working capital limit in a most efficient manner and keep the interest burden minimum. MUDRA card also helps in digitalization of MUDRA transactions and creating credit history for the borrower.

National Payments Corporation of India (NPCI) [1] has given RuPay branding to MUDRA card and also separate BIN/IIN for the same, by which credit history can be tracked. MUDRA card can be operated across the country for withdrawal of cash from any ATM/micro ATM and also for making payment through any Point-of-Sale machines.

12.6 Development and Promotional Support

Besides the credit constraints, the non-corporate small businesses (NCSBs) face many non-credit challenges, some of which are as under:

1. Skill development gaps.
2. Knowledge gaps.
3. Information asymmetry.
4. Financial/business literacy.
5. Lack of growth orientation.

To address these constraints, MUDRA adopts a credit-plus approach and offers developmental and support services to the target audience. It acts as a market-maker and build-up of ecosystem with capacities to deliver value in an efficient and sustainable manner.

12.6.1 Imparting Financial and Business Literacy: Financial/business literacy or financial education can broadly be defined as 'providing familiarity with and understanding of financial market products, especially rewards and risks, in order to make informed choices'.

Financial inclusion and financial/business literacy are twin pillars. While financial inclusion acts from supply side providing the financial market/services that people demand, financial literacy stimulates the demand side—making people aware of what they can demand. Supporting the financial literacy drive contributes substantially from the demand side to the national agenda of financial inclusion.

This apart, the micro enterprise segment also needs business literacy which will help them in acquiring knowledge on running/managing business, keeping accounts, working out ratios etc.

12.6.2 Promotion and Support of Grassroots Institutions: One of the major focus areas of MUDRA is to formalize and institutionalize the last mile financier institutions so that a new category of financial institutions, viz. small business finance companies can be created and ecosystem developed for their growth.

Rural innovations at micro enterprise/unit level are also one of the key areas for intervention and support. Support to micro units by way of the facility of incubators is taken up. This ensures that at the most grassroots levels in the country, there is climate for promotion of innovation as well as incubation of ideas from educated rural youths which would germinate in viable micro enterprises.

12.6.3 Synergies with Make in India Campaign: Government of India has initiated several steps for encouraging enterprise creation in the country. The major one is Make-in-India movement. Make in India is a major national programme designed to facilitate investment, foster innovation, enhance skill development, project intellectual property and build best in class manufacturing infrastructure. This—coupled with Start-up India and Stand-up India campaigns—has created a conducive environment of enterprise creation in different scales. MUDRA, being an initiative for promoting micro enterprises, fits well with Make-in-India initiative for supporting these micro enterprises.

12.6.4 Synergies with National Rural Livelihoods Mission (NRLM) and National Urban Livelihood Mission (NULM): NRLM aims 'to reduce poverty by enabling the poor households to access gainful self-employment and skilled wage employment opportunities, resulting in appreciable improvement in their livelihoods on a sustainable basis, through building strong grassroots institutions of the poor'. To achieve the above, NRLM, inter alia, follows a demand-driven strategy for continuous capacity building, imparting requisite skills and creating linkages with livelihood opportunities for the poor, including those emerging in the organized sector.

Similarly, NULM is another programme which is aimed at reducing urban poverty through creation of micro enterprises, individually and in group mode.

MUDRA, being an initiative for promoting micro enterprises, makes make all efforts to draw synergies between NRLM, NULM and MUDRA interventions for supporting micro enterprises and creating sustainable livelihood opportunities for the poor.

12.6.5 Synergies with National Skill Development Corporation (NSDC): NSDC is already engaged in the process of skill development at a national scale. Synergizing with NSDC will help MUDRA in augmenting the skill sets of the sectoral players.

12.6.6 Working with Credit Bureaus: With the growth of responsible lending practices, credit bureaus (CBs) have gained increasing level of acceptability in the micro finance sector. The CB culture helps in creating credit history over a period of time which will facilitate faster credit dispensation as the system evolves.

12.6.7 Working with Rating Agencies: Accreditation and rating of MFI entities is one of the roles earmarked for MUDRA. Further, a segment of financial intermediaries for the non-corporate small business sector is envisaged to emerge in the financing architecture. MUDRA works in co-ordination with rating agencies so that appropriate rating frameworks which take into account sector-specific features are devised for various sector participants. In the long-run, availability of rating for sector participants would facilitate formalization and further flow of capital to the sector.

12.7 Pricing of MUDRA Loans

Access to finance is critical and equally critical is the cost of finance to the NCSB/ultimate beneficiary. The funds mobilized by micro units from the informal sources are at a high cost. There is scope for cost rationalization. However, the rationalization is intricately linked with the cost of funds for the last mile MFIs.

While announcing the formation of MUDRA, Government of India also announced a refinance corpus for MUDRA at ₹ 20,000 crore, to be allocated by RBI from the priority sector lending shortfall. Accordingly, RBI has provided the allocation which helps in bringing down the cost of lending at the ultimate borrower level as MUDRA refinance will reduce the average borrowing cost of the lending institutions.

The NBFCs-MFIs are presently regulated by RBI and it has already prescribed detailed guidelines for margin cap in respect of MFIs. The margin cap has been pegged at 10 percent for MFIs having loan portfolio of more than ₹ 100 crore and 12 percent for smaller MFIs having loan portfolio of less than ₹ 100 crore or 2.75 times the average base rate of five major commercial banks, whichever is less. In the backdrop of these guidelines and the fact that MFI sector has been constantly trying to reduce its costs, MUDRA would also help MFIs reduce their cost to bring down the overall cost to the end beneficiaries. Further, at the time of appraisal, MUDRA would be studying/assessing individual MFIs on this as well as other related parameters and suitably price its assistance based on such assessment.

In the case of banks, RBI has also put a cap on the interest rate at base rate for lending micro units by commercial banks by availing of MUDRA refinance. Similarly, the RRBs and co-operatives have been given an interest cap of 3.50 percent over and above MUDRA refinance rate, while lending to MUDRA loan by availing of MUDRA refinance.

In case of NBFCs, RBI has also stipulated an interest cap of 6 percent over and above MUDRA refinance while their lending to MUDRA segment.

All these are expected to have a positive impact on the pricing of MUDRA loans, whereby the micro enterprises will be able to avail of credit at an affordable interest rate. However, first and foremost objective is to ensure accessibility of credit.

12.8 MUDRA in the Budget for 2018-19

Finance Minister Arun Jaitley in his budget speech to the Parliament on February 1, 2018 announced, "MUDRA Yojana launched in April, 2015 has led to sanction of ₹ 4.6 lakh crore in credit from 10.38 crore MUDRA loans. 76 percent of loan accounts are of women and more than 50 percent belong to SCs, STs and OBCs. It is proposed to set a target of ₹ 3 lakh crore for lending under MUDRA for 2018-19 after having successfully exceeded the targets in all previous years.

Non-banking finance companies (NBFCs) stepped up financing of MSMEs (micro, small and medium enterprises) after demonetization. NBFCs can be very powerful vehicle for delivering loans under MUDRA. Refinancing policy and eligibility criteria set by MUDRA will be reviewed for better refinancing of NBFCs". [2]

To sum up, MUDRA is a refinancing institution. It does not lend directly to the micro entrepreneurs/individuals. Mudra loans under Pradhan Mantri Mudra Yojana (PMMY) can be availed from nearby branch office of a bank, NBFC, MFIs etc. Borrowers can also now file online application for MUDRA loans on Mudramitra portal (www.mudramitra.in). There are no agents or middleman engaged by MUDRA for availing of Mudra loans.

Mudra loan is extended for a variety of purposes which provides income generation and employment creation in manufacturing, services, retail and agriculture-allied activities.

Endnotes

1. NPCI is an umbrella organization for all retail payments system in India. It was set up with the guidance and support of the Reserve Bank of India (RBI) and Indian Banks' Association (IBA).
2. Government of India, Ministry of Finance, Budget Papers (2018-19), *Speech of the Finance Minister*, paras 73-74.

13

Start-up India Initiative, 2016

Prime Minister Narendra Modi in his Independence Day address had announced a Start-up India initiative in which each of the 1.25 lakh bank branches would provide funding support to at least one Dalit or Adivasi entrepreneur and at least one woman entrepreneur.

Launched on January 16, 2016, Start-up India is a flagship initiative of the Government of India, intended to build a strong eco-system for nurturing innovation and Start-ups in the country that will drive sustainable economic growth and generate large scale employment opportunities. The Government through this initiative aims to empower Start-ups to grow through innovation and design.

13.1 Meaning of a Start-up

Start-up means an entity, incorporated or registered in India not prior to 5 years, with annual turnover not exceeding ₹ 25 crore in any preceding financial year, working towards innovation, development, deployment or commercialization of new products, processes or services driven by technology or intellectual property.

1. Provided that such entity is not formed by splitting up, or reconstruction, of a business already in existence.
2. Provided also that an entity shall cease to be a Start-up if its turnover for the previous financial years has exceeded ₹ 25 crore or it has completed 5 years from the date of incorporation/registration.
3. Provided further that a Start-up shall be eligible for tax benefits only after it has obtained certification from the Inter-Ministerial Board, setup for such purpose.

13.2 Start-up India: Features

In order to meet the objectives of the initiative, Government of India announced this Action Plan that addresses all aspects of the Start-up ecosystem. With this Action Plan the Government hopes to accelerate spreading of the Start-up movement:

1. From digital/technology sector to a wide array of sectors including agriculture, manufacturing, social sector, healthcare, education, etc.
2. From existing tier 1 cities to tier 2 and tier 3 cities including semi-urban and rural areas.

The Action Plan is divided across the following areas:

1. Simplification and handholding.
2. Funding support and incentives.
3. Industry-academia partnership and incubation.

13.3 Simplification and Handholding

13.3.1 Compliance Regime Based on Self-certification: The objective is to reduce the regulatory burden on start-ups thereby allowing them to focus on their core business and keep compliance cost low. Regulatory formalities requiring compliance with various labour and environment laws are time consuming and difficult in nature. Often, new and small firms are unaware of nuances of the issues and can be subjected to intrusive action by regulatory agencies. In order to make compliance for start-ups friendly and flexible, simplifications are required in the regulatory regime.

Accordingly, the process of conducting inspections shall be made more meaningful and simple. Start-ups shall be allowed to self-certify compliance (through the Start-up mobile app) with 9 labour and environment laws. In case of the labour laws, no inspections will be conducted for a period of 3 years. Start-ups may be inspected on receipt of credible and verifiable complaint of violation, filed in writing and approved by at least one level senior to the inspecting officer.

In case of environment laws, start-ups which fall under the

white category (as defined by the Central Pollution Control Board (CPCB) would be able to self-certify compliance and only random checks would be carried out in such cases.

A. Labour Laws:

1. Building and Other Constructions Workers' (Regulation of Employment and Conditions of Service) Act, 1996.
2. Inter-State Migrant Workmen (Regulation of Employment and Conditions of Service) Act, 1979.
3. Payment of Gratuity Act, 1972.
4. Contract Labour (Regulation and Abolition) Act, 1970.
5. Employees' Provident Funds and Miscellaneous Provisions Act, 1952.
6. Employees' State Insurance Act, 1948.

B. Environment Laws:

1. Water (Prevention and Control of Pollution) Act, 1974.
2. Water (Prevention and Control of Pollution) Cess (Amendment) Act, 2003.
3. Air (Prevention and Control of Pollution) Act, 1981.

13.3.2 Start-up India HUB: The purpose is to create a single point of contact for the entire start-up ecosystem and enable knowledge exchange and access to funding. Young Indians today have the conviction to venture out on their own and a conducive ecosystem lets them watch their ideas come to life. In today's environment we have more start-ups and entrepreneurs than ever before and the movement is at the cusp of a revolution. However, many start-ups do not reach their full potential due to limited guidance and access.

The Government of India has taken various measures to improve the ease of doing business and is also building an exciting and enabling environment for these start-ups, with the launch of the "Start-up India" movement.

The "Start-up India Hub" will be a key stakeholder in this vibrant ecosystem and will:

1. Work in a hub and spoke model and collaborate with Central and State governments, Indian and foreign VCs, angel networks, banks, incubators, legal partners,

consultants, universities and R&D institutions.

2. Assist start-ups through their lifecycle with specific focus on important aspects like obtaining financing, feasibility testing, business structuring advisory, enhancement of marketing skills, technology commercialization and management evaluation.
3. Organize mentorship programs in collaboration with government organizations, incubation centres, educational institutions and private organizations who aspire to foster innovation.

To all young Indians who have the courage to enter an environment of risk, the Start-up India Hub will be their friend, mentor and guide to hold their hand and walk with them through this journey.

13.3.3 Rolling-out of Mobile App and Portal: The objective is to serve as the single platform for start-ups for interacting with Government and regulatory institutions for all business needs and information exchange among various stakeholders. In order to commence operations, start-ups require registration with relevant regulatory authorities. Delays or lack of clarity in registration process may lead to delays in establishment and operations of start-ups, thereby reducing the ability of the business to get bank loans, employ workers and generate incomes. Enabling registration process in an easy and timely manner can reduce this burden significantly.

Besides, start-ups often suffer from the uncertainty regarding the exact regulatory requirements to set up its operations. In order to ensure that such information is readily available, it is intended that a checklist of required licenses covering labour licensing, environmental clearances etc. be made available. Currently, the start-up ecosystem in India also lacks formal platform(s) for start-ups to connect and collaborate with other ecosystem partners.

Towards these efforts, the Government shall introduce a mobile app to provide on-the-go accessibility for:

1. Registering start-ups with relevant agencies of the

Government. A simple form shall be made available for the same. The mobile app shall have backend integration with Ministry of Corporate Affairs and Registrar of Firms for seamless information exchange and processing of the registration application.

2. Tracking the status of the registration application and anytime downloading of the registration certificate. A digital version of the final registration certificate shall be made available for downloading through the mobile app.
3. Filing for compliances and obtaining information on various clearances/approvals/registrations required.
4. Collaborating with various start-up ecosystem partners. The app shall provide a collaborative platform with a national network of stakeholders (including venture funds, incubators, academia, mentors etc.) of the start-up ecosystem to have discussions towards enhancing and bolstering the ecosystem.
5. Applying for various schemes being undertaken under the Start-up India Action Plan.

The app shall be made available from April 1, 2016 on all leading mobile/smart devices' platforms. The start-up portal shall have similar functionalities (being offered through the mobile app) using a richer web-based user interface.

13.3.4 Legal Support and Fast-tracking Patent Examination at Lower Costs: The objective is to promote awareness and adoption of IPRs by start-ups and facilitate them in protecting and commercializing the IPRs by providing access to high quality intellectual property services and resources, including fast-track examination of patent applications and rebate in fees. Intellectual property rights (IPRs) are emerging as a strategic business tool for any business organization to enhance industrial competitiveness. Start-ups with limited resources and manpower, can sustain in this highly competitive world only through continuous growth and development oriented innovations; for this, it is equally crucial that they protect their IPRs. The scheme for Start-up Intellectual Property Protection

(SIPP) shall facilitate filing of patents, trademarks and designs by innovative start-ups. Various measures being taken in this regard include the following:

1. **Fast-tracking of Start-up Patent Applications:** The valuation of any innovation goes up immensely, once it gets the protective cover of a patent. To this end, the patent application of start-ups shall be fast-tracked for examination and disposal, so that they can realize the value of their IPRs at the earliest possible.
2. **Panel of Facilitators to Assist in Filing of IP Applications:** For effective implementation of the scheme, a panel of "facilitators" shall be empanelled by the Controller General of Patents, Designs and Trademarks (CGPDTM), who shall also regulate their conduct and functions. Facilitators will be responsible for providing general advisory on different IPRs as also information on protecting and promoting IPRs in other countries. They shall also provide assistance in filing and disposal of the IP applications related to patents, trademarks and designs under relevant Acts, including appearing on behalf of start-ups at hearings and contesting opposition, if any, by other parties, till final disposal of the IPR application.
3. **Government to Bear Facilitation Cost:** Under this scheme, the Central Government shall bear the entire fees of the facilitators for any number of patents, trademarks or designs that a start-up may file, and the start-ups shall bear the cost of only the statutory fees payable.
4. Rebate on filing of application: Start-ups shall be provided an 80 percent rebate in filing of patents vis-à-vis other companies. This will help them pare costs in the crucial formative years.

The scheme is being launched initially on a pilot basis for 1 year; based on the experience gained, further steps shall be taken.

13.3.5 Relaxed Norms of Public Procurement for Start-ups: It is meant to provide an equal platform to start-ups (in the manufacturing sector) vis-à-vis the experienced entrepreneurs and companies in public procurement. Typically, whenever a tender is floated by a Government entity or by a PSU, very often the eligibility condition specifies either *prior experience* or *prior turnover*. Such a stipulation prohibits/impedes start-ups from participating in such tenders.

Effective April 1, 2015, Central Government, State Government and PSUs have to mandatorily procure at least 20 percent from the micro, small and medium enterprises (MSMEs).

In order to promote start-ups, Government shall exempt start-ups (in the manufacturing sector) from the criteria of "prior experience/turnover" without any relaxation in quality standards or technical parameters. The start-ups will also have to demonstrate requisite capability to execute the project as per the requirements and should have their own manufacturing facility in India.

13.3.6 Faster Exit for Start-ups: Given the innovative nature of start-ups, a significant percentage fail to succeed. In the event of a business failure, it is critical to reallocate capital and resources to more productive avenues and accordingly a swift and simple process has been proposed for start-ups to wind-up operations. This will promote entrepreneurs to experiment with new and innovative ideas, without having the fear of facing a complex and long-drawn exit process where their capital remain interminably stuck.

The Insolvency and Bankruptcy Bill, 2015 (IBB), tabled in the Lok Sabha in December 2015 has provisions for the fast track and/or voluntary closure of businesses.

In terms of the IBB, start-ups with simple debt structures or those meeting such criteria as may be specified may be wound up within a period of 90 days from making of an application for winding up on a fast track basis. In such instances, an insolvency professional shall be appointed for the start-up, who shall be in charge of the company (the promoters and management shall no longer run the company) for liquidating its assets and paying its creditors within six months of such appointment. On appointment of the insolvency professional, the liquidator shall be responsible for the swift closure of the business, sale of assets and repayment of creditors in accordance with the distribution waterfall set out in the IBB. This process will respect the concept of limited liability.

13.4 Funding Support and Incentives

13.4.1 Providing Funding Support through a Fund of Funds with a Corpus of ₹ 10,000 Crore: One of key challenges faced by start-ups in India has been access to finance. Often start-ups, due to lack of collaterals or existing cash flows, fail to justify the loans. Besides, the high risk nature of start-ups wherein a significant percentage fails to take-off, hampers their investment attractiveness.

In order to provide funding support to start-ups, Government will set up a fund with an initial corpus of ₹ 2,500 crore and a total corpus of ₹ 10,000 crore over a period 4 years (i.e. ₹ 2,500 crore per year). The Fund will be in the nature of Fund of Funds, which means that it will not invest directly into start-ups, but shall participate in the capital of SEBI registered venture funds.

Key features of the Fund of Funds are highlighted below:

1. The Fund of Funds shall be managed by a Board with private professionals drawn from industry bodies, academia, and successful start-ups.
2. Life Insurance Corporation (LIC) shall be a co-investor in the Fund of Funds.
3. The Fund of Funds shall contribute to a maximum of 50 percent of the stated daughter fund size. In order to be able to receive the contribution, the daughter fund should have already raised the balance 50 percent or more of the stated fund size as the case maybe. The Fund of Funds shall have representation on the governance structure/board of the venture fund based on the contribution made.
4. The Fund shall ensure support to a broad mix of sectors such as manufacturing, agriculture, health, education, etc.

13.4.2 Credit Guarantee Fund for Start-ups: In order to

overcome traditional Indian stigma associated with failure of start-up enterprises in general and to encourage experimentation among start-up entrepreneurs through disruptive business models, credit guarantee comfort would help flow of venture debt from the formal banking system.

Debt funding to start-ups is also perceived as high risk area and to encourage banks and other lenders to provide venture debts to start-ups, credit guarantee mechanism through National Credit Guarantee Trust Company (NCGTC)/SIDBI is being envisaged with a budgetary Corpus of ₹ 500 crore per year for the next four years.

13.4.3 Tax Exemption on Capital Gains: Due to their high risk nature, start-ups are not able to attract investment in their initial stage. It is, therefore, important that suitable incentives are provided to investors for investing in the start-up ecosystem. With this objective, exemption shall be given to persons who have capital gains during the year, if they have invested such capital gains in the Fund of Funds recognized by the Government.

This will augment the funds available to various VCs for investment in start-ups.

In addition, existing capital gain tax exemption for investment in newly formed manufacturing MSMEs by individuals shall be extended to all start-ups. Currently, such an entity needs to purchase "new assets" with the capital gain received to avail such an exemption. Investment in 'computer or computer software' (as used in core business activity) shall also be considered as purchase of 'new assets' in order to promote technology driven start-ups.

13.4.4 Tax Exemption to Start-ups for 3 years: Innovation is the essence of every start-up. Young minds kindle new ideas every day to think beyond conventional strategies of the existing corporate world.

During the initial years, budding entrepreneurs struggle to evaluate the feasibility of their business idea. Significant capital investment is made in embracing ever-changing technology, fighting rising competition and navigating through the unique challenges arising from their venture. Also, there are limited alternative sources of finance available to the small and growing entrepreneurs, leading to constrained cash funds.

With a view to stimulate the development of start-ups in India and provide them a competitive platform, it is imperative that the profits of start-up initiatives are exempted from income-tax for a period of 3 years. This fiscal exemption shall facilitate growth of business and meet the working capital requirements during the initial years of operations. The exemption shall be available subject to non-distribution of dividend by the start-up.

13.4.5 Tax Exemption on Investments above Fair Market Value: Under The Income Tax Act, 1961, where a start-up (company) receives any consideration for issue of shares which exceeds the fair market value (FMV) of such shares, such excess consideration is taxable in the hands of recipient as income from other sources.

In the context of start-ups, where the idea is at a conceptualization or development stage, it is often difficult to determine the FMV of such shares. In majority of the cases, FMV is also significantly lower than the value at which the capital investment is made. This results into the tax being levied under Section 56(2) (viib) of the Act.

Currently, investment by venture capital funds in start-ups is exempted from operations of this provision. The same shall be extended to investment made by incubators in the start-ups.

13.5 India Aspiration Fund (IAF) for Start-ups

In August 2015, Government launched IAF to be set up as a fund of funds under the Small Industries Development Bank of India (SIDBI) in order to boost the start-up ecosystem in the country.

The objective of IAF is to catalyse tens of thousands of crores of equity investment into start-ups and micro, small and medium enterprises (MSMEs) creating employment of lakhs of persons, mostly educated youth, over the next four to five years.

India is witnessing a start-up revolution and to harness the potential of India's innovators and entrepreneurs, a vibrant financial ecosystem is essential. IAF will play a vital role in this financial ecosystem.

This is a well-structured fund and since it is built on sectoral allocations, it will provide investment to start-ups in sectors which are not hot today for venture funds but will become hot in future.

SIDBI under the IAF would invest in venture capital funds for meeting the equity requirement of MSME start-ups. Hence, instead of directly funding in start-ups, IAF will help the venture capitals to come up with newer investment ideas and protocols. Besides infusing crores of funding into MSMEs, this will also create lakhs of new jobs. For this, the initial corpus of ₹ 2,000 crore has been set. Life Insurance Corporation of India (LIC) will be a partner and co-investor in this fund.

The IAF is managed by an investment committee composed of captains of industry and finance.

14

Stand-up India Scheme

Scheduled castes (SCs) and scheduled tribes (STs) entrepreneurs are beginning to show great promise in starting and running successful business enterprises. The Prime Minister had given a call for promoting entrepreneurship among SCs/STs to become job providers rather than job seekers.

In the above context, the Finance Minister in his Budget Speech for the year 2016-17 remarked, "We are celebrating the 125th Birth Anniversary of Dr. B.R. Ambedkar. This must become the Year of Economic Empowerment for SC/ST entrepreneurs. We have extensively interacted with the Dalit Indian Chamber of Commerce and Industry on building an entrepreneurship ecosystem. It is proposed to constitute a National Scheduled Caste and Scheduled Tribe Hub in the MSME Ministry in partnership with industry associations. This Hub will provide professional support to scheduled caste and scheduled tribe entrepreneurs to fulfil the obligations under the Central Government procurement policy 2012, adopt global best practices and leverage the Stand-Up India initiative". [1]

14.1 Main Features of Stand-up India Scheme

The Start-up India and Stand-up India initiatives were announced by Prime Minister Narendra Modi in his address to the nation from the ramparts of Red Fort on August 15, 2015. Thereafter, the Union Cabinet approved the Stand up India Scheme in January 2016. Government of India launched the Stand-up India scheme on April 5, 2016.

The scheme facilitates bank loans between ₹ 10 lakh and ₹ 1 crore to at least one scheduled caste (SC)/scheduled tribe (ST) borrower and at least one woman borrower per bank branch for setting up greenfield enterprises. This enterprise may be in manufacturing, services or the trading sector. The scheme which is being implemented through all scheduled commercial banks is to benefit at least 2.5 lakh borrowers. The scheme is operational and the loan is being extended through scheduled commercial banks across the country.

Stand-up India scheme caters to promoting entrepreneurship amongst women, SCs and STs categories, i.e. those sections of the population facing significant hurdles due to lack of advice/mentorship as well as inadequate and delayed credit. The scheme intends to leverage the institutional credit structure to reach out to these underserved sectors of the population in starting greenfield enterprises. It caters to both ready and trainee borrowers.

Some of the features of this scheme are as under:

1. The Stand up India scheme is anchored by Department of Financial Services (DFS), Ministry of Finance to encourage greenfield enterprises by scheduled castes (SCs)/scheduled tribes (STs) and women entrepreneurs.
2. The scheme is intended to facilitate at least two such projects per bank branch, on an average, one for each category of entrepreneur.
3. The expected date of reaching the target of at least 2.5 lakh approvals is 36 months from the launch of the scheme.
4. The scheme provides for refinance window through Small Industries Development Bank of India (SIDBI) with an initial amount of ₹ 10,000 crore.
5. The scheme provides for creation of a credit guarantee mechanism through the National Credit Guarantee Trustee Company (NCGTC).
6. The scheme provides for handholding support for borrowers both at the pre-loan stage and during operations. This would include increasing their familiarity with factoring services, registration with online platforms and e-market places as well as sessions on best practices and problem solving.
7. The scheme focuses on handholding support for both

SCs/STs and women borrowers.

8. The scheme's overall intent is to leverage the institutional credit structure to reach out to these under-served sectors of the population by facilitating bank loans repayable up to 7 years and between ₹ 10 lakh to ₹ 100 lakh for greenfield enterprises in the non-farm sector set up by such SCs, STs and women borrowers.
9. The loan under the scheme would be appropriately secured and backed by a credit guarantee through a credit guarantee scheme for which Department of Financial Services would be the settler and National Credit Guarantee Trustee Company Ltd. (NCGTC) would be the operating agency.
10. Margin money of the composite loan under the scheme would be up to 25 percent. Convergence with state schemes is expected to reduce the actual requirement of margin money for a number of borrowers. Over a period of time, it is proposed that a credit history of the borrower be built-up through credit bureaus.

Endnote

1. Government of India, Ministry of Finance, *Speech of the Finance Minister, 2016-17*, para 57.

15

National Skill Development Mission (NSDM), PM Kaushal Vikas Yojana (PMKVY), and Other Initiatives

Skills and knowledge are the driving forces of economic growth and social development for any country. India currently faces a severe shortage of well-trained, skilled workers. It is estimated that only 2.3 percent of the workforce in India has undergone formal skill training as compared to 68 percent in the UK, 75 percent in Germany, 52 percent in USA, 80 percent in Japan and 96 percent in South Korea. [1]

Large sections of the educated workforce have little or no job skills, making them largely unemployable. Therefore, India must focus on scaling up skill training efforts to meet the demands of employers and drive economic growth.

India's annual skilling capacity was estimated at approximately 7 million during the period 2013-2014. Apart from meeting its own demand, India has the potential to provide a skilled workforce to fill the expected shortfall in the ageing developed world. India is one of the youngest nations in the world, with more than 54 percent of the total population below 25 years of age and over 62 percent of the population in the working age group (15-59 years). The country's population pyramid is expected to bulge across the 15-59 age group over the next decade.

This demographic advantage is predicted to last only until 2040. India therefore has a very narrow timeframe to harness its demographic dividend and to overcome its skill shortages. The enormity of India's skilling challenge is further aggravated by the fact that skill training efforts cut across multiple sectors and require the involvement of diverse stakeholders such as: (a) multiple government departments at the centre and state levels, (b) private training providers, (c) educational and training institutions, (d) employers, (e) industry associations and (f) assessment and certification bodies and trainees. All these stakeholders need to align their work together in order to achieve the target of Skill India.

15.1 Launching of Skill India Mission

National Skill Development Mission (NSDM) was approved by the Union Cabinet on July 1, 2015, and officially launched by the Prime Minister on July 15, 2015 on the occasion of World Youth Skills Day. 18,000 plus ITI graduating students received job offer letters on the occasion of World Youth Skills Day. Government has set a target to provide skill training to 40.02 crore people by 2022.

On the same day (July 15, 2015), the Prime Minister launched the following other three landmark initiatives of the Ministry of Skill Development and Entrepreneurship:

1. National Policy for Skill Development and Entrepreneurship (NPSDE), 2015.
2. Pradhan Mantri Kaushal Vikas Yojana (PMKVY).
3. Skill Loan Scheme.

NSDM has been developed to create convergence across sectors and States in terms of skill training activities. Further, to achieve the vision of Skilled India, NSDM would not only consolidate and co-ordinate skilling efforts, but also expedite decision making across sectors to achieve skilling at scale with speed and standards. It will be implemented through a streamlined institutional mechanism driven by Ministry of Skill Development and Entrepreneurship (MSDE).

The Ministry of Skill Development and Entrepreneurship (earlier Department of Skill Development and Entrepreneurship, first created in July 2014) was set up in November 2014 to drive the Skill India agenda in a Mission Mode in order to converge existing skill training initiatives and combine scale and quality of skilling efforts, with speed.

The Ministry, therefore, launched NSDM which will provide the overall institutional framework to rapidly implement and scale up skill development efforts across India. It seeks to provide the institutional capacity to train a minimum of 300 million skilled people by the year 2022.

15.2 Objectives of NSDM

NSDM seeks to:

1. Create an end-to-end implementation framework for skill development, which provides opportunities for life-long learning. This includes incorporation of skilling in the school curriculum, providing opportunities for quality long- and short-term skill training, by providing gainful employment and ensuring career progression that meets the aspirations of trainees.
2. Align employer/industry demand and workforce productivity with trainees' aspirations for sustainable livelihoods, by creating a framework for outcome focused training.
3. Establish and enforce cross-sectoral, nationally and internationally acceptable standards for skill training in the country by creating a sound quality assurance framework for skilling, applicable to all Ministries, States and private training providers.
4. Build capacity for skill development in critical un-organized sectors (such as the construction sector, where there are few opportunities for skill training) and provide pathways for re-skilling and up-skilling workers in these identified sectors, to enable them to transition into formal sector employment.
5. Ensure sufficient, high quality options for long-term skilling, benchmarked to internationally acceptable qualification standards, which will ultimately contribute to the creation of a highly skilled workforce.
6. Develop a network of quality instructors/trainers in the skill development ecosystem by establishing high quality teacher training institutions.

7. Leverage existing public infrastructure and industry facilities for scaling up skill training and capacity building efforts.
8. Offer a passage for overseas employment through specific programmes mapped to global job requirements and benchmarked to international standards.
9. Enable pathways for transitioning between the vocational training system and the formal education system, through a credit transfer system.
10. Promote convergence and co-ordination between skill development efforts of all Central Ministries, Departments, States, and implementing agencies.
11. Support weaker and disadvantaged sections of society through focused outreach programmes and targeted skill development activities.
12. Propagate aspirational value of skilling among youth, by creating social awareness on value of skill training.
13. Maintain a national database, known as the Labour Market Information System (LMIS), which will act as a portal for matching the demand and supply of skilled workforce in the country. The LMIS, will on the one hand provide citizens with vital information on skilling initiatives across the country. On the other, it will also serve as a platform for monitoring the performance of existing skill development programmes, running in every Indian state.

15.3 Institutional Mechanisms

Key institutional mechanisms for achieving the objectives of NSDM have been divided into three tiers. NSDM will consist of a Governing Council at apex level, a Steering Committee, and a Mission Directorate as the executive arm of the Mission.

Mission Directorate will be supported by three other institutions: National Skill Development Agency (NSDA), National Skill Development Corporation (NSDC), and Directorate General of Training (DGT)—all of which will have linkages with Mission Directorate to facilitate smooth functioning of the national institutional mechanism. These three agencies would continue to lie under the umbrella of Ministry of Skill Development and Entrepreneurship.

At State level, States will be encouraged to create State Skill Development Missions (SSDM) along the lines of National Skill Development Mission with a Steering Committee and Mission Directorate at State level. States will, in turn, be supported by District Committees at the functional tier.

15.4 NSDM Strategy

Seven sub-missions have been proposed initially to act as building blocks for achieving overall objectives of NSDM. They are:

1. Institutional training.
2. Infrastructure.
3. Convergence.
4. Trainers.
5. Overseas employment.
6. Sustainable livelihoods.
7. Leveraging public infrastructure.

The sub-missions can be added to/amended as per decision of Governing Council. The power to identify sub-missions in crucial areas which require immediate attention will lie with Governing Council chaired by the Prime Minister. Executive guidelines and detailing of each sub-mission will be done by Executive Committee headed by Secretary, MSDE.

Key focus areas of the sub-missions include: (a) addressing the long-term and short-term skilling needs through revamp of existing institutional training framework and establishing new institutions, (b) undertaking sector-specific skill training initiatives, (c) ensuring convergence of existing skill development programmes, (d) leveraging existing public infrastructure for skilling, (e) focusing on training of trainers, (f) facilitating overseas employment, and (g) promoting sustainable livelihoods.

Sub-Missions have currently been proposed in priority

areas. The number of sub-missions can be modified as per changing skill requirements and challenges. Each sub-mission will be headed by a Joint Secretary or Director level officer designated as CEO, sourced from the public or private sector, who has a solid track record of implementing projects and achieving targets in a timely manner. The Sub-Mission's support team will consist of high performing individuals drawn from the public and private domains.

15.5 Pradhan Mantri Kaushal Vikas Yojana (PMKVY)

On July 15, 2015, Prime Minister Narendra Modi launched the Pradhan Mantri Kaushal Vikas Yojana (PMKVY), 2015 along with the following three other landmark initiatives of the Ministry of Skill Development and Entrepreneurship:

1. National Policy for Skill Development and Entrepreneurship, 2015.
2. National Skill Development Mission.
3. Skill Loan Scheme.

The slogan *Kaushal Bharat, Kushal Bharat* suggests that skilling Indians (*Kaushal Bharat*) will result in a happy, healthy, prosperous and strong nation (*Kushal Bharat*).

PMKVY is the flagship, demand-driven, reward-based skill training scheme of the Ministry of Skill Development and Entrepreneurship (MSDE). It is intended to incentivise skill training by providing financial rewards to candidates who successfully complete approved skill training programmes. For the first time, the skills of young people who lack formal certification, such as workers in India's vast unorganised sector, will be recognised. Through an initiative known as recognition of prior learning (RPL), 10 lakh youth will be assessed and certified for the skills that they already possess.

Under PMKVY, skill cards and skill certificates are awarded which allow trainees to share their skill identity with employers. Each skill card and skill certificate features a quick response code (QR Code), which can be read through a QR reader on mobile devices. Trainees can use these to share their skill qualifications with employers in a quick and reliable way during the job search process.

Approved for another four years (2016-2020) to benefit 10 million youth, training and assessment fees under PMKVY are completely paid by the Government.

15.5.1 Key Components of the Scheme: These are as under:

A. Short-term Training: Short-term training imparted at PMKVY Training Centres (TCs) is expected to benefit candidates of Indian nationality who are either school/college dropouts or unemployed. Apart from providing training according to the National Skills Qualification Framework (NSQF), TCs shall also impart training in soft skills, entrepreneurship, financial and digital literacy. Duration of the training varies per job role, ranging between 150 and 300 hours. Upon successful completion of their assessment, candidates shall be provided placement assistance by Training Partners (TPs). Under PMKVY, the entire training and assessment fees are paid by the Government. Payouts shall be provided to the TPs in alignment with the Common Norms. Trainings imparted under the short-term training component of the scheme shall be NSQF Level 5 and below.

B. Recognition of Prior Learning: Individuals with prior learning experience or skills shall be assessed and certified under the Recognition of Prior Learning (RPL) component of the scheme. RPL aims to align the competencies of the unregulated workforce of the country to the NSQF. Project Implementing Agencies (PIAs), such as Sector Skill Councils (SSCs) or any other agencies designated by MSDE/NSDC, shall be incentivized to implement RPL projects in any of the three project types (RPL Camps, RPL at Employers Premises and RPL Centres). To address knowledge gaps, PIAs may offer Bridge Courses to RPL candidates.

15.5.2 Special Projects: The special projects component of PMKVY envisages the creation of a platform that will facilitate trainings in special areas and/or premises of Government bodies, corporates or industry bodies, and trainings in special job roles not defined under the available Qualification Packs (QPs)/National Occupational Standards (NOSs). Special projects are projects that require some deviation from the terms and conditions of short-term training under PMKVY for any stakeholder. A proposing stakeholder can be either Government institutions of Central and State Government(s)/Autonomous Body/Statutory Body or any other equivalent body or corporates who desire to provide training to candidates.

15.5.3 Kaushal and Rozgar Mela: Social and community mobilisation is extremely critical for the success of PMKVY. Active participation of the community ensures transparency and accountability, and helps in leveraging the cumulative knowledge of the community for better functioning. In line with this, PMKVY assigns special importance to the involvement of the target beneficiaries through a defined mobilisation process. TPs shall conduct Kaushal and Rozgar Melas every 6 months with press/media coverage. They are also required to participate actively in National Career Service Melas and on-ground activities.

15.5.4 Placement Guidelines: PMKVY envisages to link the aptitude, aspiration, and knowledge of the skilled workforce it creates with employment opportunities and demands in the market. Every effort thereby needs to be made by the PMKVY TCs to provide placement opportunities to candidates, trained and certified under the Scheme. TPs shall also provide support to entrepreneurship development.

15.5.5 Monitoring Guidelines: To ensure that high standards of quality are maintained by TCs, NSDC and empanelled inspection agencies shall use various methodologies, such as self-audit reporting, call validations, surprise visits, and monitoring through the Skills Development Management System (SDMS). These methodologies shall be enhanced with the engagement of latest technologies.

The scheme will be implemented through the National Skill Development Corporation (NSDC).

In his speech while presenting the Budget for 2017-18 to the

Parliament, the Finance Minister Arun Jaitley observed, "*Pradhan Mantri Kaushal Kendras* (PMKK) have already been promoted in more than 60 districts. We now propose to extend these *Kendras* to more than 600 districts across the country. 100 India International Skills Centres will be established across the country. These Centres would offer advanced training and also courses in foreign languages. This will help those of our youth who seek job opportunities outside the country.

In 2017-18, we also propose to launch the Skill Acquisition and Knowledge Awareness for Livelihood Promotion (SANKALP) programme at a cost of ₹ 4,000 crore. SANKALP will provide market relevant training to 3.5 crore youth.

The next phase of Skill Strengthening for Industrial Value Enhancement (STRIVE) will also be launched in 2017-18 at a cost of ₹ 2,200 crore. STRIVE will focus on improving the quality and market relevance of vocational training provided in ITIs and strengthen the apprenticeship programmes through industry cluster approach". [2]

15.6 Udaan

Udaan is a Special Industry Initiative for Jammu and Kashmir (J&K) in the nature of partnership between the corporates of India and Ministry of Home Affairs and implemented by National Skill Development Corporation. The programme aims to provide skills training and enhance the employability of unemployed youth of J&K. The scheme covers graduates, postgraduates and three year engineering diploma holders. It has two objectives:

(a) To provide an exposure to the unemployed graduates to the best of Corporate India.

(b) To provide Corporate India, an exposure to the rich talent pool available in the State.

The key stakeholders are:

- Ministry of Home Affairs (MHA): Chief Benefactors.
- State Government (Jammu and Kashmir).
- Corporates: Training Partners.

- Implementation Agency: NSDC.

The scheme aims to cover 40,000 youth of J&K over a period of 5 years and a sum of ₹ 750 crore has been earmarked for implementation of the scheme over a period of 5 years to cover other incidental expenses such as travel cost, boarding and lodging, stipend and travel and medical insurance cost for the trainees and administration cost. Further corporates are eligible for partial reimbursement of training expense incurred for the candidates who have been offered jobs.

15.7 Skill Loan Scheme

Launched on July 15, 2015, the scheme will make available loans ranging from ₹ 5,000-₹ 1.5 lakh to 34 lakh youth of India seeking to attend skill development programmes over the next 5 years.

15.8 National Apprenticeship Training Scheme (NATS)

Apprenticeship is a time-tested way of learning a craft or trade under a Master Craftsman. Apprenticeship training is a procedure where young, technically qualified people undergo training under a master trainer to become equipped for jobs in the modern scenario. It has the double benefit of earning while learning. Apprenticeship is an agreement between a person (an apprentice) who wants to learn a skill and an employer who needs a skilled worker. The apprentices are taught the latest applications, processes and methodologies in their respective fields of work from some of the most renowned organisations in India. This also acts as a transition phase for a school/ college student from classroom to a working background. The apprentice also learns soft skills, work culture, ethics and organisational behaviour while undergoing training. This goes a long way in helping him/her secure permanent employment in the future. At the end of training they are issued a certificate attesting to their training and proficiency in a particular field. This serves as an experience certificate when they seek employment after their training.

NATS, sponsored by Ministry of Human Resource Development, Government of India, is a one year programme equipping technically qualified youth with practical knowledge and skills required in their field of work. The apprentices are imparted training by the organizations at their place of work. Trained managers with well- developed training modules ensure that apprentices learn the job quickly and competently. During the period of apprenticeship, the apprentices are paid a stipend amount, 50 percent of which is reimbursable to the employer from Government of India. At the end of the training period the apprentices are issued a certificate of proficiency by Government of India which can be registered at all employment exchanges across India as valid employment experience. The apprentices are placed for training at Central, State and private organizations which have excellent training facilities. NATS is one of the flagship programmes of Government of India for skilling Indian youth.

15.9 Deen Dayal Upadhyaya Grameen Kaushalya Yojana (DDU-GKY)

The Ministry of Rural Development (MoRD), Government of India announced DDU-GKY on September 25, 2014. DDU-GKY is a part of the National Rural Livelihood Mission (NRLM), tasked with the dual objectives of adding diversity to the incomes of rural poor families and cater to the career aspirations of rural youth.

DDU-GKY is uniquely focused on rural youth between the ages of 15 and 35 years from poor families. As a part of the Skill India Campaign, it plays an instrumental role in supporting the social and economic programmes of the Government like Make in India, Digital India, Smart Cities, Start-up India, and Stand-up India campaigns.

National Policy for Skill Development and Entrepreneurship, 2015 has identified a skills gap of 109.73 million in 24 key sectors by the year 2022. This presents an unprecedented opportunity for India to train its youth population and place them in jobs across the world and realize its demographic dividend.

Innovation from partners is encouraged to build scale and capacity. Its unique implementation structure involves partners, who are by nature, committed to changing lives and are experts in their areas. They form a part of the skilling ecosystem integrated by DDU-GKY. Partners are supported through investment, capacity building, strategies for retention, linkages to international placement and technology support for training purposes.

Endnotes

1. Government of India, Ministry of Skill Development and Entrepreneurship, *National Skill Development Mission: A Framework for Implementation*, 2015, p. 2.
2. Government of India, Ministry of Finance, Budget Papers 2017-18, *Speech of the Finance Minister*, paras 54 to 56.

16

National Career Service (NCS) Project

India's economy has grown impressively in recent years. The country is poised to grow even faster, with its demographic potential, high investment and savings rates, and allocation of resources for infrastructure. But its high pace of economic growth and notable progress in reducing poverty over the last decade contrasts with the persistent gaps in creating a more inclusive, productive and formal labour market. Investment in skills development will ensure that economic and employment growth is more inclusive. This is especially important in the context of India's demographic transition that has also produced a youth bulge in the working age population.

India has a significant advantage of a young population and a declining dependency ratio, offering huge potential for a demographic dividend. There are, however, challenges which need to be addressed for fully reaping this unique dividend in the global scenario. Although the annual rate of growth of the Indian economy is one of the highest in the world, the growth in jobs is much less than the growth of the economy.

National Career Service (NCS) project is an initiative of the Ministry of Labour and Employment, Government of India for establishing quick and efficient career-related services.

Prime Minister Narendra Modi launched the National Career Service programme on July 20, 2015 at the Forty-sixth Labour Conference with an objective of supporting varied stakeholders with better career information, easily available jobs and other employment-related services. Its vision is to provide a national platform for interface between stakeholders for responsive, transparent and efficient employment services in order to meet skill needs of a dynamic economy. The NCS programme is accessible through web and provides a large number of employment-related services to the Indian citizens. These services are supported by a toll free number 1800-425-1514 and are accessible through a network of common service centres and model career centres etc. It provides various career-related services like job search, career counselling, information on skill training programs/career options, job postings, organizing and participating in job fairs, finding blue collared local service providers (LSPs) like plumbers, electricians etc.

The key success factors of NCS initiative revolve around strengthening the existing employment exchange ecosystem with an ICT-enabled platform and reaching out to masses through multiple delivery channels and partnerships with existing job market players. Caught in a vicious cycle of decreasing job seeker registrations and vacancy notifications by employers, employment exchanges needed a transformation for better delivery of employment services. Employment exchanges have been transformed to focus more on counselling-related needs of candidates with establishment of career centres.

NCS is the converging point for Government of India's three major initiatives, namely Skill India, Digital India and Make in India, that aim to provide skilled manpower, improve digital infrastructure and generate employment opportunities for all.

16.1 Key Aspects of the NCS Project

With this background, NCS has been conceptualized as a comprehensive, multi-pronged, transformational project. Key aspects of this project include the following:

1. Establishment of career centres which would be enabled by making the right infrastructure and linkages available to perform counselling functions.
2. Implementation of a comprehensive capacity building initiative for augmenting the skills of career centre professionals and other ecosystem counselling partners.
3. Setting up a National Portal which will act as a platform to

bridge the gap between Government and private job providing ecosystem, job seeker and skill development ecosystem.

4. Providing access to tools to analyse skill-wise demand of industry and supply of jobseekers, as well as access to a rich knowledge repository of career counselling content in multiple languages so that candidates are counselled appropriately.
5. Collaboration with various stakeholders like State Governments, schools, colleges, jobseekers, skill development institutions, employers, NGOs, volunteer agencies, technology partners, verification agencies etc.
6. Establishing institutional/governance structures and revenue model for securing sustainability and relevance of the services being offered through these centres.
7. Appropriate information, education and communication (IEC) strategies to reach out to the stakeholders.

16.2 Focus Areas

NCS initiative aims to address the gaps in the employment market by strategic interventions for improving decent employment, enhancing quality of workforce, enhancing female labour force participation, entrepreneurial endeavours, informal to formal transition, engaging with rural workforce for higher productivity, and re-employment (second life) opportunities etc.

The focus areas for the NCS platform are listed below:

1. Enhancing career and employment opportunities.
2. Counselling and guidance for career development.
3. Focusing on decent employment.
4. Enhancing quality of workforce.
5. Enhancing female labour force participation.
6. Encouraging entrepreneurial endeavours.
7. Focusing on inclusive growth initiatives.
8. Engaging with rural workforce for higher productivity.
9. Re-employment opportunities for returning and retired workforce.

10. Transition of workforce from informal to formal sectors.

The above list is indicative (and not exhaustive) and the Central Government may add to this list from time-to-time based on the needs of the economy and society for improving the employment market. Specific interventions could be designed on the NCS for one or more of the above focus areas.

16.3 Services Offered

Under the NCS initiative, the NCS Portal (www.ncs.gov.in) will be the platform where the various stakeholders will be interacting for exchange of career and employment-related opportunities. The counsellors empanelling with the Directorate General of Employment (DGE), Ministry of Labour and Employment, will offer the various services through this platform and leverage the network of career centres (employment exchanges) in the delivery of these services some of which are listed below:

1. **Online Registration of Candidates.**

- PAN/Aadhaar-based verification.
- Search for vacancies, counsellors etc.
- Rich repository of career content.
- Participation in job fairs.
- Seeking counselling and guidance services.

2. **Online Registration of Establishments.**

- Posting and managing job vacancies.
- Search for skilled workforce.
- Participation in job fairs.

3. **Online Registration of Counsellors and Guidance Experts**

- PAN/Aadhaar-based verification.
- Providing counselling/guidance services.

4. **Online Registration of Local Service Providers (Plumbers, Drivers, Electricians etc.)**
5. **Multiple Delivery Channels**

- Employment exchanges (career centres).
- Common service centres (CSCs).

- Internet and mobile-based access.

6. **Value Added Services Like Updates, Notifications, Alerts through SMS, E-mail, and IVRS etc.**
7. **Multi-lingual Call Centre (1800-425-1514) Services for Helping Candidates and Establishments in Registration, Profile Updation etc.**

16.4 Career Counselling

The Government is now giving increased focus on career counselling as a key activity of NCS to enable aspiring youth to pursue the right career choice according to their aptitude so that they join the workforce with better skills for enhancing growth and development. It has a vision to develop Career Centres as a real exchange platform for job seekers and providers. There is also a need to evolve a road map to make these centres tie-up with educational institutions and potential industries.

NCS aims to create a network of career counsellors on the NCS platform where the career centres will be the hub of counselling services. The services will include administration of psychometric tests to assess the student's/job seeker's personality/aptitude/interest etc. These tests would be made available via both online and offline modes. The NCS Portal provides an opportunity to browse through the list of the approved counsellors and book an appointment with them. Counselling services would be made available on face-to-face basis or via online platforms depending upon the chosen medium. The main aim of career counselling is to assist the job seekers in choosing a field that is in tune with their skills and their career expectations. The NCS Project also envisages offering vocational guidance services through empanelled vocational guidance (VG) experts, having requisite experience and expertise.

An integral component of the NCS Project is the establishment of model career centres (MCCs) in collaboration with the States. MCCs will have adequate facilities and infrastructure for delivery of various services to the stakeholders and can be subsequently replicated at other locations.

The NCS makes available a rich repository of career content on over 3,000 occupations across 52 sectors. The services under NCS are available online and can be accessed directly, through career centres, common service centres, mobile devices, cyber cafes etc. A dedicated helpdesk (multi-lingual) is also available from Tuesday to Sunday on 1800-425-1514 from 8.00 a.m. to 8 p.m. for assisting users.

16.5 Career Centres

NCS Project is focussed on establishing career centres in a phased approach ensuring that standardized set of services are offered all across.

16.5.1 Objectives: Career centres will connect local youth and other job-seekers with all possible job opportunities in a transparent and effective manner through the use of technology as well as through counselling and training. While the state-of-the-art technology driven National Career Service Portal will, in a sustained manner, provide information about available job opportunities and resources for career centres to function effectively, the career centres would be the pivotal outreach and counselling interface of the National Career Service for teeming millions of aspiring youth from rural, semi-urban areas as well as from disadvantaged sections of the society.

These centres would be staffed by motivated and competent personnel, enabled with necessary tools and infrastructure for accomplishing the following purposes:

1. Effectively and continuously assessing demand of skills in labour markets, local in other States and abroad.
2. Guiding youth visiting the centres or by outreach to schools/colleges, various training institutions, about the training, on-the-job training, job opportunities etc. according to their aptitude and potential.
3. Connecting youth and other job seekers with jobs through portal, job fairs and other possible interface with employees

such as campus placements.

4. Mobilizing employers and other placement agencies to connect to NCS for meeting their HR requirements.

16.5.2 Services Offered through Career Centres: Career centres will be responsible for all activities related to the NCS project and will be linked to the NCS portal services for improved quality of services and outcomes. Activities to be performed by career centres can be categorized as follows:

A. Coverage (Catchment Area): Each Career Centre would cater to a catchment area comprising around 3-4 adjacent districts covering an area of approximately 100 square kilometres to map out the availability of institutions, industry, demographics etc. and post the details on the NCS portal for general access. The catchment area is for the purpose of capturing information on the portal in a comprehensive manner and is not intended to deny access of services to any candidate. The Ministry of Labour and Employment would facilitate model career centres in conducting demand and supply assessment survey.

B. Demand Side (Industry Interaction): Career centres will undertake market sizing exercise to estimate the number of employment opportunities in their area, associated skill requirements, skill training capacity availability etc. This will require close and constant interface with local industry and employers.

C. Supply Side (Candidate Engagement): On the supply side, career centres will provide counselling services to the job seekers and make them aware of opportunities based on their skills, area of interest and requirement. Career centres will thus provide a range of employment related services like career counselling, job matching, employment market analytics and other value added services.

D. Job and Skill Mapping: Career centres will undertake the job skill mapping for identification of right fit job for candidate. The candidates will be assessed through skill assessment and psychometric tests and guided to the right opportunity whether it is for employment, skill training, apprenticeship training, on-the-job-training, finishing course (gap training) etc.

E. IEC Activities: Career centres will through multi-pronged IEC strategy increase awareness amongst the various stakeholders like skill training institutes, assessment bodies, schools and college administration, local community leaders, government departments and public in general about the services available.

F. Last Mile Employability Courses: The Ministry is evolving a scheme for offering last mile employability courses for enhancing the employability of youth. These courses will be made available through selected institutions after approval of the scheme and will be rolled out through the model career centres.

17

Direct Benefit Transfer (DBT) Mechanism

To bring a paradigm shift in the delivery of services to the citizens, particularly common man and the under-privileged section of society of the country, the Government took a decision to start the technology-driven DBT mechanism.

17.1 Roll Out of the Programme

Pursuant to the decision taken in the meeting of the National Committee on Direct Cash Transfers held by the Prime Minister, DBT was rolled out from January 1, 2013 in 43 districts for 26 selected Central Sector and Centrally-sponsored Schemes in a phase-wise manner beginning with 20 districts on January 1, 2013, 11 districts from February 1, 2013 and the remaining 12 districts from March 1, 2013. Subsequently, the DBT rollout was further scaled up in a phase-wise manner in other districts.

Phase II of DBT was launched from July 1, 2013 in 78 identified districts. Three additional schemes were identified for DBT. The districts were identified on the basis of sufficient Aadhaar enrolment figures and financial inclusion. The schemes were selected on the basis of higher incidence of beneficiaries with bank accounts and where flow of funds was found to be relatively simpler. Accordingly, most schemes are related to scholarships, benefits to women and child labour.

Thus, benefits such as scholarships, pensions, and Mahatma Gandhi National Rural Employment Guarantee Scheme (MGNREGS) wages are directly credited to the bank or post office accounts of identified beneficiaries.

DBT is designed to improve targeting, reduce corruption, eliminate waste, control expenditure, and facilitate reforms. Transfers that were taking place through paper and cash mode are now done through electronic transfers. This has been enabled by rapid roll out of Aadhar (Unique Identity). DBT in tandem with such unique identification has ensured that the benefits reach the target groups faster and minimize inclusion and exclusion errors as well as corruption that are associated with manual processes.

All public sector banks (PSBs) and regional rural banks (RRBs) have made provision so that the data collected by the Departments/Ministries/Implementing agency concerned can be used for seeding the bank account details in the core banking system (CBS) of banks with Aadhaar. All PSBs have also joined the Aadhaar Payment Bridge of the National Payments Corporation of India (NPCI) for smooth transfer of benefits.

17.2 Prerequisites for Execution of DBT

These are as under:

1. Digitization of database of beneficiary with Aadhaar number.
2. Opening of bank accounts of beneficiaries.
3. Enrolment of beneficiaries for generation of Aadhaar numbers.
4. Digitized database to be seeded with Aadhaar number.
5. Bank Accounts to be seeded with Aadhaar number.

17.3 Advantages of DBT

DBT provides the following advantages:

1. Consolidated cash transfers to households which are getting benefits from multiple sources and multiple forms.
2. Improve efficiency of social safety net, consolidated income support programme for the poor and eliminate multiple sources of subsidy.
3. Positive institutional externalities.
4. Adoption of cutting edge technical system.
5. Free administrative system from exercise of control to focus on development.
6. Maximize benefits from expenditure of welfare schemes

which leads to overall human development.

DBT is primarily meant for under-privileged and weaker sections of the society. DBT has been launched in North Eastern States and is operational in Tripura and Sikkim. Various welfare schemes for scheduled castes (SCs), scheduled tribes (STs), other backward classes (OBCs), women, children, senior citizens and disabled have been included in DBT mechanism.

17.4 Disadvantages of DBT

These can be listed as follows:

1. Value of transfers may be inadequate, especially if they are not indexed to market prices and inflation.
2. Access to banks/ATMs and markets may vary across locations.
3. Recipients may use cash for non-specified purposes, negating the purpose of subsidy

To sum up, DBT has emerged as an important mechanism for transfers to citizens under different welfare/subsidy schemes of Government and in future its scope is likely to enlarge substantially. DBT has helped in efficient processing of the transfers and weeding out ghost beneficiaries.

18

Need for Inclusive Growth

A major weakness in the economy is that the growth is not perceived as being sufficiently inclusive for many groups, especially scheduled castes (SCs), scheduled tribes (STs), and minorities. Gender inequality also remains a pervasive problem and some of the structural changes taking place have an adverse effect on women. The lack of inclusiveness is borne out by data on several dimensions of performance.

18.1 Inclusive Growth Defined

Inclusive growth may be defined as growth that promotes equal opportunities and increases access to these opportunities, i.e. growth that allows all members of society to participate in and contribute equally to development efforts, regardless of individual circumstances. This concept appears in Asian Development Bank's (ADB) *Strategy 2020* that examines the extent of inequality of opportunities and to what extent it can be overcome by different types of growth process. The main idea in the ADB's approach is to focus on productive employment as an important element of inclusive growth.

Inclusive growth, defined in a broader sense has three dimensions:

1. Equity among all sections of the society.
2. Equity among all sectors of the economy.
3. Equity among all regions in the country.

Thus, inclusive growth means inter-group, inter-sector as well as inter-regional equity. Growth is inclusive when it creates economic opportunities along with ensuring equal access to them.

Inclusive growth is different from poverty reduction, where the focus is on re-distributing wealth and making transfers through public expenditure activities. In poverty reduction, the poor are primarily passive recipients of donation. In inclusive growth, the objective is to enable the poor with the opportunities to empower them in a better way.

Inclusive growth is the new mantra of national and international agencies like United Nation Development Programme (UNDP) and the World Bank. UNDP defines inclusive growth—by laying emphasis on the production and income side of the GDP—as "the process and the outcome where all group of people have participated in the organization of growth and have benefited equitably from it. Thus, inclusive growth represents an equation with organization on the left hand side and benefits on the right hand side".

Inclusiveness means many different things and each aspect of inclusiveness poses its own challenges for policy.

18.1.1 Inclusiveness as Poverty Reduction: Distributional concerns have traditionally been viewed as ensuring an adequate flow of benefits to the poor and the most marginalised. This must remain an important policy focus. It is worth noting that the record in this dimension of inclusiveness is encouraging. The percentage of the population below the official poverty line has been falling but even as that happens, the numbers below the poverty line remain large.

18.1.2 Inclusiveness as Group Equality: Inclusiveness is not just about bringing those below an official fixed poverty line to a level above it. It is also about a growth process which is seen to be 'fair' by different socio-economic groups that constitute our society. The poor are certainly one target group, but inclusiveness must also embrace the concern of other groups such as the scheduled castes (SCs), scheduled tribes (STs), other backward classes (OBCs), minorities, the differently-abled and other marginalised groups. Women can also be viewed as a disadvantaged group for this purpose. These distinct 'identity groups' are sometimes correlated with income slabs—the SCs and STs, for example, are in the lower income category—and all poverty alleviation strategies help them directly. Women on the other hand span the entire income spectrum, but there are gender-based issues of inclusiveness that are relevant all along the spectrum.

18.1.3 Inclusiveness as Regional Balance: Another aspect of inclusiveness relates to whether all States, and indeed all regions, are seen to benefit from the growth process. The regional dimension has grown in importance in recent years. On the positive side, many of the erstwhile backward States have begun to show significant improvement in growth performance and the variation in growth rates across States has narrowed. However, both the better performing and other States are increasingly concerned about their backward regions, or districts, which may not share the general improvement in living standards experienced elsewhere. Many of these districts have unique characteristics including high concentration of tribal population in forested areas, or minorities in urban areas. Some districts are also affected by left wing extremism, making the task of development much more difficult.

An important constraint on the growth of backward regions in the country is the poor state of infrastructure, especially road connectivity, schools and health facilities and the availability of electricity, all of which combine to hold back development. Improvement in infrastructure must therefore be an important component of any regionally inclusive development strategy.

18.1.4 Inclusiveness and Inequality: Inclusiveness also means greater attention to income inequality. Perfect equality is not found anywhere and there are many reasons why it may not even be a feasible objective. However, there can be no two opinions on the fact that inequality must be kept within tolerable limits. Some increase in inequality in a developing country during a period of rapid growth and transformation may be unavoidable and it may even be tolerated if it is accompanied by sufficiently rapid improvement in the living standards of the poor. However, an increase in inequality with little or no improvement in the living standards of the poor is a recipe for social tensions. Static measures of inequality do not capture the phenomenon of equality of opportunity which needs special attention. Any given level of inequality of outcomes is much more socially acceptable if it results from a system which provides greater equality of opportunity. As a society, we therefore need to move as rapidly as possible to the ideal of giving every child in India a fair opportunity in life, which means assuring every child access to good health and quality education.

18.1.5 Inclusiveness as Empowerment: Inclusiveness is not just about ensuring a broad-based flow of benefits or economic opportunities, it is also about empowerment and participation. It is a measure of the success achieved in building a participatory democracy that people are no longer prepared to be passive recipients of benefits doled out by the Government. They are slowly beginning to demand these benefits and opportunities as rights and they also want a say in how they are administered. This brings to the fore issues of governance, accountability and peoples' participation to much greater extent than before. This also covers areas like access to information about government schemes, knowledge of the relevant laws and how to access justice. The growing concern with governance has also focused attention on corruption.

Each of the dimensions of inclusiveness discussed above is relevant, and public attention often focuses on one or the other at different times. The aim should be to achieve steady progress in each of these dimensions. Accelerated growth in recent years has yielded distinct benefits to many and the prosperity which this has generated is visible to all, raising the expectations of all sections of the population, and creating a demand for a fair share of the benefits of growth. Policymaking has to be watchful of developments in each dimension of fairness and be quick to take corrective steps as soon as the need arises.

18.2 Strategy for Inclusive Growth

According to the Eleventh Five Year Plan (2007-12), "The strategy for achieving faster growth with greater inclusiveness involves several interrelated components. These are: (i) a continuation of the policies of economic reform which have created a buoyant and competitive private sector capable of benefiting from the opportunities provided by greater integration with the world, (ii) a revival in agricultural growth which is the most important single factor affecting rural prosperity, (iii) improved access to essential services in health and education (including skill development) especially for the poor, which is essential to ensure inclusiveness and also to support rapid growth, (iv) a special thrust on infrastructure development which is a critical area for accelerating growth, (v) environmental sustainability which is becoming increasingly important, (vi) special attention to the needs of disadvantaged groups, and (vii) good governance at all levels, Central, state, and local.

As in most market economies, the dominant impulse for growth will come from the private sector. India is fortunate in having a strong private sector capability ranging from agriculture, which is entirely dependent on private farmers, most of whom have modest land holdings, through small and medium entrepreneurs in industry and services to larger domestic corporate entities, many of which benefit from FDI to varying degrees. The Eleventh Plan must ensure a policy environment that is supportive of this vibrant and globalized private sector which has an important contribution to make in India's future development.

Emphasizing the importance of the private sector is not to downplay the role of the government. On the contrary, apart from the usual role of government in providing a stable macroeconomic policy, the Eleventh Plan envisages a very large role for public policy in a number of sectors". [1]

Financial inclusion of all individuals and all sections of population is very vital from the point of view of ensuring inclusive growth of the national economy. Adoption and implementation of inclusive practices by all banks and financial institutions and also by insurance companies and mutual funds will go a long way in bringing about financial inclusion of all those who presently stand financially excluded. Financial inclusion refers to the process of bringing into the financial and banking fold all those who are outside and giving them opportunities to utilize various banking and financial services at affordable cost.

Inclusive growth calls for higher degree of attitudinal transformation of individuals, institutions, administrative and governing agencies towards concern and commitment for work coupled with ethical and social values of development. Good governance, more then policies and reforms, is the key to achieving inclusive growth by translating outlay into outcome.

Liberalization of the Indian economy has no doubt resulted in rapid economic growth but has also led to increased income inequalities. Therefore, the very objective of inclusive growth is defeated if the poor do not benefit from the economic growth.

Inclusive economic growth can achieved by focusing on expanding the regional scope of economic growth, expanding access to assets and thriving markets and expanding equity in the opportunities for the next generation of Indian citizen no matter whom they are or where they live.

Although the government is taking various steps for the welfare of the poor and weaker sections of the society, measures cannot prove to be effective as long as the institutional delivery system is weak. Further, the Government alone cannot do all the things as the scale of resources is limited. Therefore, corporates should also take initiatives for the socio-economic development of the disadvantaged groups.

The objective of inclusiveness can be achieved, *inter alia*, through the following:

1. Reduction of regional imbalances.
2. Support to institutions located in border, hilly, remote, small towns, and educationally backward areas.
3. Support to institutions with larger student population of SCs, STs, OBCs, minorities, and physically challenged.
4. Support to the SCs, STs, OBCs, minorities, physically

challenged, and girl students with special scholarships and fellowships, hostel facilities, remedial coaching, and other measures.

18.3 Target Groups for Inclusive Growth: These include the following:

1. Scheduled tribes including particularly vulnerable tribal groups.
2. Scheduled castes.
3. Nomadic tribes and de-notified tribes.
4. Fisher folk.
5. Hand using legacy artisans.
6. Isolated communities (away from habitations).
7. Households of manual scavengers.
8. Households of bonded labourers.
9. Women headed/managed households (single, divorced, deserted, widows).
10. Households with person/persons with disability.
11. Households with elderly but with no persons in the age group of 16-59 years.
12. Destitute households.
13. Shelterless households.
14. Households involved in daily wage labour.
15. Households with migrant labour.
16. Households with people working in hazardous occupations.
17. Households having persons living with HIV and AIDS.
18. Communities affected by/displaced by natural calamities/development projects.
19. Households displaced out and communities living in difficult areas.

For growth to be more inclusive, the following are required: (a) better performance in agriculture, (b) faster creation of jobs, especially in manufacturing, (c) stronger efforts at health, education and skill development, (d) improved effectiveness of programmes directly aimed at the poor, (e) special programmes for socially vulnerable groups, and (f) special plans for disadvantaged/backward regions.

18.4 Enabling Role of the State for Inclusive Growth

For achieving inclusive growth there is critical need to rethink the role of the state. The early debate among economists about the size of the Government can be misleading. The need of the hour is to have an *enabling* Government. India is too large and complex a nation for the state to be able to deliver all that is needed. Asking the Government to produce all the essential goods, create all the necessary jobs, and keep a curb on the prices of all goods is to court failure, and lead to a large, cumbersome bureaucracy and widespread corruption. The aim must be to stay with the objective of inclusive growth that was laid down by the founding fathers of the nation, but to take a more modern view of what the state can realistically deliver. This is what leads to the idea of an enabling state—a Government that does not try to directly deliver to the citizens everything that they need. Instead, it creates an enabling environment for the market so that individual enterprise can flourish and citizens can provide for the needs of one another. Besides, government steps in to help those who do not manage to do well for themselves, because there will always be individuals, irrespective of the system, who need support and help.

Therefore, the need is for a government which, when it comes to the market, sets effective, incentive-compatible rules and remains on the sidelines with minimal interference. At the same time, it plays an important role in directly helping the poor by ensuring that they get basic education and health services and receive adequate nutrition and food. This rollback of the Government in the former will enable it to devote more energy and resources to and be more effective in the latter.

The Government of India has much to deliver as it tries to reconcile India's vast socio-economic inequalities. The need of the hour is to strengthen the following key enablers of inclusive growth: (a) infrastructure inclusion, (b) global inclusion, (c) financial inclusion, (d) digital inclusion, (e) talent and social inclusion, and (f) agriculture productivity upgradation. These are the key enablers which can play a significant role in the promotion of inclusive growth in India.

Inclusive strategy involves a much greater role of the States, and closer coordination between the Centre and the States, than would be needed for a purely corporate-led growth strategy. This is because most of the policy measures and institutional support required for small and medium entrepreneur-led growth lie in the domain of State Governments and local bodies. The Centre's contributions would lie mainly in creating the appropriate macroeconomic framework, financial sector policies and national level infrastructure.

To sum up, the growth in India has been pro-rich and pro-urban to a larger extent. The financial sector has had urban bias and globalization intensified this, as the macro policies have not been pro-employment and pro-poor in India.

India has the potential of becoming a leading economy and has the unique opportunity to make that growth inclusive, provided that there is willingness on the part of all sections of society to put in hard and disciplined work, together with serious, sustained and purposeful planning.

Growth with justice is the cornerstone of the Indian planning so that every household and each individual gets the benefits of the economic growth. That is the reason so much of emphasis is being placed on the inclusiveness of the economic growth. The nature of economic growth in terms of inclusiveness implies, inter alia, putting more people in productive and sustainable jobs.

Inclusive growth is the new paradigm that is related essentially to equality and opportunity to all and sundry for productive and meaningful life with freedom and equality. There is a lot of talk on growth and equity but there is no operational plan. An immediate plan for achieving equitable development is urgently needed. The challenge before the Government is to evolve a system in which reforms and globalization can proceed on one track, and the poor can be protected from the ill effects of it, on the other. Local communities and markets should be reinforced to take advantage of finance, trade and investment changes flowing from the national and global levels. Investing to improve productivity in agriculture is essential for sustainable poverty reduction. There is no globalization without successful localization.

Endnote

1. Government of India, Planning Commission, *Eleventh Five Year Plan* (2007-12), Volume I, Preface.

Bibliography

Bibliography

Acharya, S.S. and G.F. Papanek (1995), "Explaining Agricultural Wage Trends in India", *Development Policy Review*, Volume 13, No. 1, March.

Bhalla, S. (2000), "Behind Poverty: The Quantitative Dimension of Employment Prospects for Rural Indians", Working Paper Number 7, Institute for Human Development, New Delhi.

Chadha, G.K. and Alakh N. Shanna (eds.) (1997), "Growth, Employment and Poverty: Change and Continuity in Rural India", Vikas Publishing House Pvt. Ltd., New Delhi.

Dreze, Jean and Amartya Sen (2002), "India: Development and Participation", Oxford University Press, New Delhi.

Dutta, B. and B. Ramaswami (2001), "Targeting and Efficiency in the Public Distribution System", *Economic and Political Weekly*, Volume 36, May.

Fan, S., P. Hazell, S. Thorat (2000), "Government Spending, Growth, and Poverty in Rural India", *American Journal of Agricultural Economics,* 82(4):1038-1051.

Fisher, Thomas and M.S. Sriram (2000), "Beyond Micro-credit: Putting Development Back into Micro-finance", Vistaar Publications, New Delhi.

Ghosh, M. (1996), "Agricultural Development and Rural Poverty in India", *Indian Journal of Agricultural Economics,* Volume 51.

Government of India, Ministry of Social Justice and Empowerment, *Annual Report* (various years).

——Ministry of Tribal Affairs, *Annual Report* (various years).

——Ministry of Minority Affairs, *Annual Report* (various years).

——Ministry of Panchayati Raj, *Annual Report* (various years).

——Ministry of Rural Development, *Annual Report* (various years).

——Ministry of Women and Child Development, *Annual Report* (various years).

——Ministry of Finance, *Budget Papers* (various years).

—— Ministry of Finance, *Economic Survey* (various years).

—— Ministry of Law, Justice, and Company Affairs, *Constitution of India.*

Himanshu, M. and A. Sen (2011), "Why not a Unified Food Security Legislation?", *Economic and Political Weekly,* Volume 46,

April.

Joshi, Sandeep (2000), "Panchayat Raj Institutions and Poverty Alleviation", Rawat Publications, Jaipur.

Kalpana, K. (2005), "Shifting Trajectories in Micro Finance Discourse", *Economic and Political Weekly*, Volume XL No. 51.

Klaauw, B.V. and Limin Wang (2004), "Child Mortality in Rural India", World Bank, Washington DC.

Minhas, B.S., L.R. Jain and S.D. Tendulkar (1991), "Declining Incidence of Poverty in the 1980s: Evidence vs. Artefacts", *Economic and Political Weekly,* Volume 26, July 6-13.

Narasimhan, Sankuntala (1999), "Empowering Women: An Alternative Strategy from Rural India", Sage Publications, New Delhi.

Planning Commission of India (2004), "Unlocking the Potential: National Strategy for Accelerated Poverty Reduction", General Economics Division, December.

Pradhan, K.B., P.K. Roy, M.R. Sailaja and S. Venkataraman (2000), "Rural-Urban Disparities: Income Distribution, Expenditure Pattern and Social Sector", *Economic and Political Weekly,* Volume 35, July 15.

Purushothaman, Sangeetha (1998), "The Empowerment of Women in India: Grassroots Women's Networks and State", Sage Publications, New Delhi.

Radhakrishna, R. (2002), "Food and Nutrition Security", in Kirit S. Parikh and R. Radhakrishna (eds.), 'India Development Report', Oxford University Press, New Delhi.

Radhakrishna, R., K. Hanumantha Rao, C. Ravi, B. Sambi Reddy (2004), "Chronic Poverty and Malnutrition in 1990s", *Economic and Political Weekly,* July 10.

Rajaraman, Indira (2005), "Financing Rural Infrastructure in Developing Countries", *Applied Econometrics and International Development,* Volume 5.

Rajasekhar, D. (2000), "Non-government Organizations (NGOs) in India: Opportunities and Challenges", *Journal of Rural Development*, Volume 19, No. 2.

Rao, Hanumantha C.H. (1999), "Changing Economic Structure of the Rural Economy in Asia and the Pacific", paper presented at the study meeting on Rural Transformation, held at Yogakarta, Indonesia, November 29 to December 3.

Ravallion, Martin (2000), "What is Needed for a More Pro-Poor

Growth Process in India", *Economic and Political Weekly*, Volume 35, March 25-31.

Ray, R. (2000), "Poverty, Household Size and Child Welfare in India", *Economic and Political Weekly*, September 23.

Reserve Bank of India, *Bulletin* (various issues).

——*Handbook of Statistics on Indian Economy* (various years).

——*Report on Currency and Finance* (various years).

Saith, A. (1981), "Production, Prices and Poverty in Rural India", *Journal of Development Studies*, Volume 17, No. 2.

Sangwan, S.S. (1998), "Emerging Issues of Indian Peasantry", *Yojana*, October, Volume 42 No. 10.

Sharma, S.S.P. (2003), "Development Programmes, Environment and Rural Poverty in India", *Journal of Rural Development*, Volume 22.

Shetty, S.L. (2003), "Credit Flows to Rural Poor", mimeo, EPW Research Foundation, Mumbai.

Subramanian, S. (2011), "Inclusive Development and the Quintile Income Statistic", *Economic and Political Weekly,* Volume 46, January 22.

Svedberg, P. (2011), "Reforming or Replacing the Public Distribution System with Cash Transfers?", *Economic and Political Weekly*, Volume 47, February 18.

Thorat, Sukhadeo (2004), "Persistence of Poverty: Why do Scheduled Castes and Scheduled Tribes Stay Chronically Poor?", Working Paper for Centre for Chronic Poverty, London.

Tripathi, S.N. (1996), "Unorganised Women Labour in India", Discovery Publishing House, New Delhi.

Vaidyanathan, A. (2001), "Poverty and Development Policy", *Economic and Political Weekly*, May 26.

Viswanath, Vanita (1993), "NGOs and Women's Development in Rural South India: A Comparative Analysis", Vistaar Publications, New Delhi.

World Bank (2003), "India: Sustaining Reform, Reducing Poverty", A World Bank Development Policy Review, Oxford University Press.

Websites

Ministry of Social Justice and Empowerment

Ministry of Tribal Affairs

Ministry of Minority Affairs

Ministry of Women and Child Development
Ministry of Rural Development
Ministry of Panchayati Raj
Ministry of Finance
Reserve Bank of India
National Bank for Agriculture and Rural Development
NITI Aayog

Index

Index